Board of State Viticultural Commissioners

## The Vineyards in Sonoma County

Being the Report of I. De Turk, Commissioner for the Sonoma District

Board of State Viticultural Commissioners

**The Vineyards in Sonoma County**
*Being the Report of I. De Turk, Commissioner for the Sonoma District*

ISBN/EAN: 9783337157517

Printed in Europe, USA, Canada, Australia, Japan

Cover: Foto ©ninafisch / pixelio.de

More available books at **www.hansebooks.com**

THE

# VINEYARDS IN SONOMA COUNTY;

BEING

## THE REPORT OF I. DeTURK, COMMISSIONER
## FOR THE SONOMA DISTRICT,

TO THE

## BOARD OF STATE VITICULTURAL COMMISSIONERS OF CALIFORNIA.

PUBLISHED BY THE BOARD OF STATE VITICULTURAL
COMMISSIONERS.

SACRAMENTO:
STATE OFFICE, : : : : : A. J. JOHNSTON, SUPT. STATE PRINTING.
1893.

# THE VINEYARDS OF SONOMA COUNTY.

## REPORT OF I. DeTURK,

### Commissioner for the Sonoma District.

SANTA ROSA, June 30, 1893.

*To the Board of State Viticultural Commissioners:*

GENTLEMEN: I herewith submit the report of Allen B. Lemmon, Esq., on the condition of the vineyards of Sonoma County, and the census of the same, as obtained by him under my direction, together with the report of Winfield Scott, Secretary, on the scope of the work and the recapitulation of the figures obtained.

Respectfully submitted.

I. DeTURK,
Commissioner for the Sonoma District.

## REPORT OF WINFIELD SCOTT.

SAN FRANCISCO, June 30, 1893.

*Hon.* I. DeTURK, *Commissioner for the Sonoma District:*

· SIR: At your request I have prepared a recapitulation of the census of Sonoma County made under your direction. As with the work prosecuted in Napa, Alameda, and Santa Clara Counties, the following blank was used:

................................................ County.

................................................ District in County.

Name and address,----------------------------------------------------------------

Total acres in vines,------------------------------------------------------------

Acres in bearing,----------------------------------------------------------------

Acres in wine grapes,------------------------------------------------------------

Acres in table grapes,-----------------------------------------------------------

Acres in raisin grapes,----------------------------------------------------------

Will be replanted, and how many acres,-------------------------------------------

Acres at present infested by Phylloxera.  { Good for only one crop more, ------ acres.
Total, ------acres.  { Good for more than one crop more, ----acres.

Acres planted to resistants.  { Riparia, ---------- acres.
Total,------acres.  { Rupestris, -------- acres.
  { Lenoir, ---------- acres.
  { Other varieties, -------- acres.

On Riparia, ------acres.  { Which varieties succeed best?--------
  { Which varieties have not succeeded?--------
On Rupestris, ------acres.  { Which varieties succeed best?--------
  { Which varieties have not succeeded?--------
On Lenoir, ------acres.  { Which varieties succeed best?--------
  { Which varieties have not succeeded?--------
On other varieties (name  { Which varieties succeed best?--------
them), ------acres.  { Which varieties have not succeeded?--------

Acres planted to Resistants (same  { Grafted and in bearing, ----acres.
as preceding).  { Grafted and not bearing, ----acres.
Total,------acres.  { Not yet grafted, ----------acres.

Character of the soil of the vineyard:-------------------------------------------

How is the vineyard situated—low lying, upland, or mountain?--------------------

What is exposure to sun and wind?-----------------------------------------------

Which of the European varieties have proved most resistant?---------------------

How have the vineyards that have been attacked been handled?--------------------

Crop in 1892?-------------------------------------------------------------------

Stock of wine on hand, in gallons?----------------------------------------------

Total quantity of cooperage, ----------gallons:  { Oak cooperage,------------gallons.
  { Redwood cooperage,----------gallons.

Remarks:------------------------------------------------------------------------

The returns tabulated are as follows:

TOTAL IN SONOMA COUNTY.

Total number of vineyards_____832.
Total acreage in vines_____23,291½ acres.
Acreage in bearing_____21,908½ acres.
Acreage in wine grapes_____22,613 acres.
Acreage in table grapes_____664½ acres.
Acreage in raisin grapes_____14 acres.
Infested by phylloxera_____801 acres.
Same good for but one crop more_____328 acres.

Planted to resistants_____2,328½ acres { Riparia __ _____278 acres.
Rupestris _____None.
Lenoir _____289 acres.
Other _____136 acres.
Variety not named _____Balance.

Planted to resistants_____2,328½ acres { Grafted and bearing _____684½ acres.
Grafted but not bearing_____108 acres.
Not yet grafted _____9 acres.
Not reported_____Balance.

Crop in 1892 _____48,409¾ tons.
Cooperage_____7,676,300 gallons { Oak _____2,595,000 gallons.
Redwood _____5,081,300 gallons.

The recapitulation of the districts in the county is as follows:

FIRST DISTRICT.

*Comprising Vallejo and Sonoma Townships.*

Number of vineyards_____136.
Total acreage in vines_____5,535½ acres.
Acreage in bearing_____4,942½ acres.
Acreage in wine grapes_____5,182½ acres.
Acreage in table grapes_____353 acres.
Infested by phylloxera_____782 acres.
Same good for only one more crop_____328 acres.

Planted to resistants_____1,186 acres { Riperia_____265 acres.
Rupestris_____None.
Lenoir _____259 acres.
Other varieties_____136 acres.
Unspecified ____ _____526 acres.

Planted to resistants_____1,186 acres { Grafted and in bearing_____550 acres.
Grafted but not bearing _____108 acres.
Not grafted _____ 48 acres.
Unspecified_____Balance.

Crop in 1892 _____ 5,870½ tons.
Cooperage_____2,840,000 gallons { Oak _____877,000 gallons.
Redwood _____1,963,000 gallons.

SECOND DISTRICT.

*Comprising Analy and Petaluma Townships.*

Number of vineyards_____97.
Total acreage in vines_____1,869 acres.
Acreage in bearing_____1,841 acres.
Acreage in wine grapes_____1,835½ acres.
Acreage in table grapes_____32½ acres.
Acreage in raisins_____1 acre.
Crop in 1892 _____5,000 tons.
Cooperage _____267,050 gallons { Oak _____42,050 gallons.
Redwood _____225,000 gallons.

THIRD DISTRICT.

*Comprising Santa Rosa and Russian River Townships.*

Number of vineyards_____384.
Total acreage in vines_____7,894 acres.
Acreage in bearing_____7,406 acres.
Acreage in wine grapes_____7,145½ acres.
Acreage in table grapes_____148½ acres.
Infested by phylloxera_____18 acres.
Planted to resistants (not specified)_____6 acres.
Crop in 1892 _____16,572½ tons.
Cooperage _____1,663,300 gallons { Oak _____800,800 gallons.
Redwood _____ _____862,500 gallons.

## FOURTH DISTRICT.

*Comprising Cloverdale, Mendocino, Knights Valley, and Washington.*

| | |
|---|---|
| Number of vineyards | 282. |
| Total acreage in grapes | 7,241 acres. |
| Acreage in bearing | 6,987 acres. |
| Acreage in wine grapes | 7,105½ acres. |
| Acreage in table grapes | 123½ acres. |
| Acreage in raisin grapes | 12 acres. |
| Infested by phylloxera | 1 acre. |

Planted to resistants ____ 136½ acres {
Riparia __ 13 acres.
Rupestris __ None.
Lenoir __ 30½ acres.
Unspecified __ Balance.

Planted to resistants ____ 136½ acres {
Grafted and bearing __ 134½ acres.
Grafted but not bearing __ None.
Not yet grafted __ 2 acres.

| | |
|---|---|
| Crop in 1892 | 19,327 tons. |

Cooperage ____ 2,260,500 gallons {Oak __ 398,200 gallons.
{Redwood __ 1,862,300 gallons.

## FIFTH DISTRICT.

*Comprising the Townships of Bodega, Ocean, Redwood, and Salt Point.*

| | |
|---|---|
| Number of vineyards | 33. |
| Total acreage in vines | 752 acres. |
| Acreage in bearing | 732 acres. |
| Acreage in wine grapes | 744 acres. |
| Acreage in table grapes | 7 acres. |
| Acreage in raisin grapes | 1 acre. |
| Crop in 1892 | 1,640 tons. |

Cooperage ____ 646,450 gallons {Oak __ 476,950 gallons.
{Redwood __ 169,500 gallons.

Respectfully submitted.

WINFIELD SCOTT,
Secretary.

## REPORT OF ALLEN B. LEMMON.

SANTA ROSA, CAL., June 20, 1893.

*Hon. I. DeTurk, Viticultural Commissioner for the Sonoma District:*

DEAR SIR: Herewith I submit my report of the canvass of Sonoma County in the collection of vineyard and wine statistics, as per blank forms furnished by you for such purpose.

In doing this work, I first sent a circular letter to all vineyardists, with a blank form and addressed stamped envelope for the reply, asking for the desired information. This was preliminary to the general visitation of the county, and thus I secured a showing from about two hundred vineyardists. This was followed by visitation to every neighborhood and to almost every vineyard.

The statistics have been collected and classified by supervisor districts, of which there are five. After careful study of the county, this seemed to me to be the most satisfactory division of the territory. The first district includes the Sonoma Valley, in which phylloxera has done the greatest damage, with some contiguous country. The vineyards about Sebastopol, in Analy Township, and the few vineyards about Petaluma constitute the second district. The third district is composed of Santa Rosa and Russian River Townships; the fourth of the Healdsburg country and the territory north and east of there, and the fifth the coast region of the county.

Much attention has been given to the vineyards infested by phylloxera. In some instances the patience of the owners has been wearied by the questions asked. It was ascertained that in some instances high fertilization and very thorough cultivation were tried, but the ravages of the disease continued just the same. One or two flooded their vineyards with water, where it could be done, but this did not tend to check the deadly work of the disease. Bisulphide of carbon was tried, but it proved too expensive, and is not known to have done much good. Such efforts to save vineyards were exceptional cases. Most grape growers have made no effort whatever at special treatment, either digging out the infested vineyard and planting the ground to something else, or replanting with resistants as the old vines have died.

From the best information obtainable, I conclude that the first appearance of phylloxera in this county was in the Dresel-Gundlach vineyard, a few miles south of Sonoma, in 1874 or 1875. There, much money was expended on suggested remedies and in experimenting with resistants. In time all the old vines were destroyed and resistants took their place, and the vineyard is now in a very flourishing condition.

From this old and noted vineyard the phylloxera has extended north some twenty miles. At Glen Ellen it crossed over into Bennett Valley some five or six years ago, through which it has entered northward several miles. Three years ago the disease made its appearance in the Upper Russian River Valley, in the vineyards of L. G. Ellis and C. P. Moore. These vineyards are about three miles apart, and the river flows between them. Mr. Ellis can offer no explanation for the appearance of the insects in his vineyard, unless it was brought there with some cuttings received from a district in which phylloxera has since shown itself. Mr. Moore shipped some of his grapes to a winery in an infested district a few years ago, and he thinks the troublesome insect may have been carried to his home in the boxes returned. There are one or two other vineyards in the neighborhood of that of Mr. Moore in which a considerable number of vines have died, but the owners attribute the loss to other causes.

The work of destruction is very apparent in the extensive vineyard owned by J. G. Fair in Vallejo Township. One field of nearly forty acres is badly infested, and a single spot of a few rods square was found in a neighboring vineyard.

In all other sections of the county the vines were found to be healthy, except an occasional touch of black knot. The people owning vineyards on the deep sandy loam that predominates in Analy Township are quite hopeful that vines in soil of that character are safe from attacks of phylloxera, but those cultivating the heavier loams do not speak with as much confidence. Within a few days, men who pronounced their vines healthy two months ago have reported the recent appearance of phylloxera in their vineyards.

In the Sonoma Valley a considerable number of resistant vineyards have been planted, but many old vineyards have disappeared and their owners have abandoned the culture of the grape. In other portions of the county there is much talk of turning attention to other crops. Grape growers are generally much discouraged—some on account of the ravages of the phylloxera, and others at the low prices which have long prevailed. While a few have added somewhat to their vineyards and are hoping that the day is not distant when grape growing will be again profitable, the greater number are discouraged.

As will be seen by examination of the detailed report submitted, many more Riparia have been planted than any other of the resistant variety. While these vines are slower growers than some others, they are generally regarded as the most reliable. As most of the resistant vineyards are young, just coming into bearing, it has not been possible to get much information in regard to results. At the same time, it may be said that there is great confidence that resistant vineyards will be permanent, and that in the near future they are likely to be profitable.

In attempting to grow resistant vineyards, there have been some mistakes in grafting. It will not do to graft too low. If this is done the grafts are likely to throw out roots, and in time take the place of the resistant root. This is followed by phylloxera killing the vine, and thus all the work and expense have been for naught. It seems settled that the graft should be put in at about the surface of the ground. There is difference of opinion as to the kind of grafting best to apply to the grape, as will be seen by examination of the remarks of some of the vineyardists.

While phylloxera has done great harm in portions of this county, it is gratifying to note the many large and important districts in which the vines are still healthy and give promise of good returns. In journeying about the county, not nearly as many infested vineyards were found as had been reported. With great valleys as well as large areas of upland entirely free from phylloxera or other disease, after its existence in parts of the county for many years, it would seem likely that the prominence of this section for grape growing and wine making will long be maintained.

The increased acreage of table grapes is noted. Also, that this crop is usually quite profitable. There are a considerable number of such vineyards, and more are being planted every year.

While the report shows returns from 832 vineyards, aggregating 23,-291½ acres, with a yield last year of 48,409¾ tons, there are many small vineyards of less than five acres which have not been reported. It is believed that there are at least one hundred of these, whose aggregate acreage is certainly 250.

The winery returns are not as complete as would be desirable, but the best has been done. Some wine makers have declined to give any figures, and others have made statements that were afterward found to be incorrect. In some instances two letters were written without getting any returns, and afterward, on visiting the winery, nobody was found there who was able to give the particulars asked for.

The collection of these statistics was not an unpleasant task. Most grape growers were found to be very reasonable and accommodating. After frankly talking the matter over with them, not more than a half dozen declined to answer the questions asked to the best of their ability. In doing this work the writer has had opportunity to meet in a friendly way and talk a few minutes with most of the men in this county engaged in this important industry. This has given me a knowledge of their business that could have been secured in no other way, and in submitting this report I return thanks to you for the favor you bestowed in permitting me to make this canvass.

Respectfully submitted.

ALLEN B. LEMMON.

# REPORT ON VINEYARDS.

# FIRST DISTRICT.

*Agnew, S. J., Sonoma.*—Total, 15 acres; all in bearing; soil light loam; slopes slightly to the south; crop, 10 tons.

*Aguillon, A., Sonoma.*—Total, 7 acres; infested by phylloxera, 3 acres; planted to resistants (Lenoir), 4 acres; soil light adobe and gravelly; low lying; south exposure; crop, 2 tons.

*Akers, M. P., Shellville.*—Between 4 and 5 acres; all in bearing; soil black loam; valley or low lying land; crop, 11 tons.

*Batto, John, Sonoma.*—Total, 25 acres; in bearing, 18 acres; infested by phylloxera, 18 acres; all good for one more crop; light gravelly soil; low lying; southern exposure; crop, 30 tons. An old vineyard at the north side of Sonoma Valley. There have been 7 acres planted to resistants—3 to Riparia and 4 to Lenoir. The resistant vines are not yet in bearing.

*Bell, Mrs. Teressa, Glen Ellen.*—Total, 75 acres; in bearing, 75 acres; all infested by phylloxera, but apparently good for one more crop; soil light gravelly, part of the tract being upland and part mountain; southern and western exposure; crop, about 50 tons. This is the former J. H. Drummond place of 150 acres, once planted to superior foreign varieties and noted for its vineyard. It is now badly infested by phylloxera, half the vineyard, or 75 acres, being entirely gone, and the other half near the end of its existence. It is proposed to clean up the entire vineyard after this year and use the land for other purposes.

*Bihler, William, Lakeville.*—Total, 15 acres; in bearing, 12 acres; soil reddish land and light adobe; upland; western exposure. A young vineyard near San Pablo Bay, the last crop being only 10 tons.

*Black, Mrs. J. W., Petaluma.*—Total, 7 acres; all in bearing and all wine grapes; soil gravelly loam; summit of Sonoma Mountain; southeast exposure; crop estimated at about 12 tons.

*Boletti, V., Sonoma.*—Total, 18 acres; in bearing, 12 acres; infested by phylloxera, 12 acres, but all good for more than one crop; planted to resistants (Lenoir), 6 acres; soil black loam; low lying; southern exposure; crop, 12 tons.

*Bassaca, Frank, Glen Ellen.*—Total, 16 acres; in bearing, 6 acres; infested by phylloxera, 16 acres; all good for one more crop; soil red gravelly; upland; southern exposure; crop, 6 tons.

*Bowen, John D., Glen Ellen.*—Total, 8 acres; all in bearing; all infested by phylloxera—the remnant of an old vineyard; soil red gravel; mountain; exposure in all directions; crop, 45 tons; no wine on hand; cooperage, 10,000 gallons oak and 5,000 gallons redwood. This vineyard is at the northern end of Sonoma Mountain and is 1,700 feet above sea-level.

*Bowen, John, Glen Ellen.*—Total, 20 acres; all in bearing; all infested by phylloxera; good for one more crop; soil gravelly black loam; mountain; south and east exposure; crop, 40 tons. This vineyard is on the mountains near the Napa County line. Half of it has been killed by phylloxera.

*Boyes, Capt. H. E., Glen Ellen.*—Total, 5 acres; all in bearing; of this vineyard 1½ acres have been planted to Lenoir vines; soil dark loam; low lying; southeast exposure; crop, 20 tons. This vineyard is now but one third the size it was at the making of the last report.

*Breitenbach, F., Sonoma.*—Total, 6 acres; all in bearing; all infested by phylloxera, 4 acres being considered good for one more crop and 2 acres for a longer time; gravelly loam; low lying; level land, fully exposed to wind and rain; has done nothing with infested vines, but expects to take them out and plant the land to something else; crop, about 6 tons.

*Burgess, P. B., Sonoma.*—Total, 8 acres; planted to resistants (Riparia), but not in bearing; soil red gravelly; low lying; southern exposure; wine on hand, 7,000 gallons; cooperage, 100,000 gallons, of which 40,000 is oak and 60,000 is redwood.

*Burris, Mrs. E., Sonoma.*—Total, 40 acres; not in bearing; planted to wine grapes, 20 acres; to table grapes, 20 acres; all on resistant (Riparia) stocks; soil light loam; low lying; southern exposure. This vineyard was destroyed by phylloxera, and an equal number of acres have been planted with resistant stocks.

*Cady, M. K., Agua Caliente.*—Total, 25 acres; all in bearing, and all planted to wine grapes; all infested by phylloxera, 15 acres being good for one more crop, and 10 acres for more than one crop; planted to resistants (Lenoir), 3 acres; soil light gravelly, part being alluvial and part adobe; low land; southwest exposure; crop, 60 tons; wine on hand, 7,000 gallons; cooperage, 30,000 gallons, half being oak and half redwood. This vineyard formerly consisted of 50 acres, half of which died out and the vines were dug up. The Tokays and Isabellas were not affected by phylloxera and they remain strong and healthy.

*California Home for Feeble-Minded Children, Glen Ellen.*—Total, 50 acres; in bearing, 40 acres; wine grapes, 5 acres; table grapes, 45 acres; infested by phylloxera, 15 acres, good for one more crop; planted to resistants (Riparia), 10 acres, grafted but not in bearing; soil light clay and gravel; part low lying and part upland; north and west exposure; crop, 50 tons.

*Campbell, B. F., Sonoma.*—Total, 21 acres; in bearing, 16 acres; acres in wine grapes, 10; in table grapes, 10; infested by phylloxera, 10 acres, all good for one more crop; planted to resistants (Lenoir), 10 acres, half of which is grafted and in bearing, the other 5 acres being grafted but not in bearing; soil black loam; low lying; southern exposure; crop, 40 tons. This vineyard is north of the town of Sonoma and in the valley of the same name. In this locality the Tokay grape ripens well and colors most satisfactorily.

*Carpenter & Gilchrist, South Los Guilicos.*—Total, 20 acres; in bearing, 15 acres; wine grapes, 18 acres; table grapes, 2 acres; infested by phylloxera, 10 acres, all good for more than one crop; soil light clay; mountain; southern and eastern exposure; crop, 25 tons. This vineyard is high up on the mountain, near the Napa and Sonoma County line.

*Charles, E. L., Lakeville.*—Total, 20 acres; in bearing, 20 acres, of which 18 acres are wine and 2 acres table grapes; no disease noted; soil adobe loam; upland; southwest exposure; crop, 27 tons, only 9 acres being in bearing last year.

*Chauvet, J., Glen Ellen.*—Total, 12 acres; all in bearing, but most of the vines have been taken by phylloxera; have been putting in resistant roots as the other vines have died out; soil gravelly loam; upland; eastern exposure; crop, 6 tons; stock of wine on hand about 100,000 gallons; cooperage, 200,000 gallons, half being oak and half redwood.

*Clark, Mrs. C., South Los Guilicos.*—Total, 108 acres; all in bearing, and all wine grapes; soil red gravel and black loam; part lowland and part hills; southern exposure; crop, 250 tons. This vineyard lies at the base of mountains just north of the village of Kenwood, or South Los Guilicos, and is one of the best in the valley.

*Clark, Geo., Glen Ellen.*—Total, 5 acres; Tokays; crop, 10 tons.

*Clarke, Robert, Agua Caliente.*—Total, 20 acres; in bearing, 10 acres; all planted to resistants (Riparia), half of which have been grafted and are now in bearing; soil black loam; low lying; southern exposure; crop, 18 tons. This was formerly a vineyard of 25 acres, but phylloxera wholly destroyed it and 20 acres have been replanted, as stated above.

*Cooper, J. S. and J. R., Sonoma.*—Total, 7 acres; in bearing, 3 acres; table grapes, 4 acres; wine grapes, 3 acres; infested by phylloxera, 3 acres, which have been replanted to Lenoir, but have not yet been grafted; soil rich alluvial; low lying; full exposure; crop, 10 tons.

*DeTurk, I., Santa Rosa.*—Total, 125 acres; in bearing, 100 acres; all wine grapes; infested by phylloxera, 100 acres, of which 40 acres are good for only one more crop and 60 acres for more than another crop; all to be replanted with resistants; now planted to resistants (Riparia), 25 acres, not yet grafted; soil red gravelly loam; rolling upland, the exposure being to all points of the compass; is not certain as to the most resistant European varieties; has given the attacked vines very little special attention, pulling them out when they have become much diseased; crop, 64 tons; stock of wine on hand, 500,000 gallons; cooperage, 640,000 gallons, of which 90,000 gallons is oak and 550,000 gallons redwood.

This vineyard was planted in 1884, 1885, and 1886. Mr. DeTurk has had much experience in growing grapes and making wine. More than thirty years ago he started the noted Yulupa vineyard, now the property of G. W. Davis, and he gave close study and attention to the grape and wine business. His new vineyard ground was selected as being superior in all respects, and only the best and most approved varieties of wine grapes were planted. Just after the young vineyard came into bearing, some four or five years ago, the phylloxera appeared. It first attacked the Chauché Noir varieties, and it now affects all varieties of vinifera. The crop was not much affected by the disease until last year.

*Dowdell & Son, El Verano.*—Total, 10 acres; in bearing, 10 acres; all wine grapes; red soil; low lying; northern exposure; crop, 20 tons.

*Drahms, Augustus, San Quentin* (vineyard near Sonoma).—Total, 25 acres; in bearing, 22 acres; wine grapes, 10 acres; table grapes, 15 acres; infested by phylloxera, 3 acres; good for only one more crop, 2 acres; good for more than another crop, 20 acres; planted to resistants, 15 acres, of which 9 acres is Riparia and 6 acres other varieties; grafted and in bearing, 9 acres; Zinfandel and Chasselas grafted on Riparia succeed best; of

Tokays on their own roots there are 6 acres, partly but not wholly resistant, but will not do on soil in which the disease exists, as they grow slowly and sometimes bear, but finally succumb; soil light sandy loam; slightly rolling; westerly exposure; infested vines have been taken up and Riparia and Lenoir vines have been put in; crop, 30 tons. Mr. Drahms has great faith in resistant stocks. He thinks it a question of but a few years when all other vineyards will be dead, and that then those planted to resistant roots will become very valuable.

*Dresel, Carl, Sonoma.*—Total, 45 acres; acres in bearing, 23; all in wine grapes; acres in resistants, 45; all resistants, except a few, Lenoir and Elvira; soil volcanic, some lime, chalk, and gravelly loam; upland; southwestern exposure; crop, 90 tons; made 13,000 gallons of wine last year.

*Dresel & Co., Sonoma.*—Total, 85 acres; all wine grapes; 60 acres in bearing; all resistants, the phylloxera having taken the entire old vineyard—Riparia, 75 acres; Lenoir, 5 acres; Elvira, 4 acres; Taylor, 1 acre; grafted and in bearing, 60 acres; grafted and not in bearing, 25 acres; all varieties succeed well on resistant stocks, especially the Riparia; great variety of soil, gravelly, light, and sandy loam; upland; southwest exposure; none of the European varieties proved resistant; made from home vineyard, 37,000 gallons of wine; entire vintage, 115,000 gallons; stock of wine on hand, 250,000 gallons; cooperage, 359,000 gallons, of which 295,000 gallons is oak and 64,000 gallons is redwood.
The two Dresel vineyards, that of Mr. Gundlach and of the Henry Winkle estate, constitute the famous purchase of 1857 by the elder Dresel and his associates, with some additions since secured. Phylloxera attacked these vineyards in 1874 and 1875. In 1878 experiments with resistants were begun. The Taylor and Riparia were the first tried. Since then all resistants have been tried in these vineyards, and all the leading varieties of wine grapes have been used as grafts. Mr. Dresel has least confidence in the Taylor and Elvira. The vineyards on the Dresel and Gundlach places show superior care and cultivation, the vines being vigorous and entirely healthy. The winery is supplied with water from an artesian well, which was secured after almost a fortune had been spent on experiments.

*Duerson, John, Penn's Grove.*—Total, 8 acres; all in bearing, and all wine grapes; gravelly loam; mountain; northeast exposure; crop, 8 tons.

*Dunn, T. M., Sonoma.*—Total, 40 acres; nearly all dead, killed by phylloxera; has planted 10 acres of resistants, half each of Riparia and Lenoir; all grafted, but not yet in bearing; soil light gravel; low lying; southern exposure; no crop worth considering.

*Emfiaran, Mrs. Lulu Vallejo, Sonoma.*—Total, 25 acres; acres in bearing, 25, of which 20 acres are wine and 5 are table grapes; infested by phylloxera, 1 acre, which will be good for but one more crop; 24 acres appear healthy; soil very fertile alluvial; low lying; southern exposure; crop, 30 tons. About 70 acres of Zinfandel and Mission grapes on this place died in the ten years from 1878 to 1888.

*Engler, George, Sonoma.*—Total, 12 acres; all wine grapes and just beginning to bear; all resistants (Lenoir); grafted; soil black loam; low lying; southern exposure; no crop reported; stock of wine on hand, 3,000 gallons; cooperage, 20,000 gallons, half being oak and half redwood.

*Erskine & Hinshaw, Sonoma.*—Total, 36 acres; in bearing, 20 acres; wine grapes, 5 acres; table grapes, 31 acres; a part of the old Haraszthy vineyard, all the old vines having been killed by phylloxera; resistants, 5 acres (Riparia), the other varieties occupying 31 acres; soil red gravel; low lying; southern and western exposure; crop, 7 tons, the vineyard having just begun bearing.

*Ewell Estate, Sonoma.*—Total, 20 acres; all table grapes; the young vines just coming into bearing; red soil; low lying; southern exposure; crop, 9 tons.

*Fair, Jas. G., Lakeville.*—Total, 300 acres; all in wine grapes; in bearing, 300 acres; infested by phylloxera, 38 acres; good for only one more crop, 10 acres; good for more than another crop, 28 acres; some replanting to resistants where other vines have died out; soil black loam, gravel, and adobe; upland; south and west exposure; crop, 600 tons; stock of wine on hand, 550,000 gallons; cooperage, 600,000 gallons, all reported as redwood.
This is the former William Bihler place. Until within the past year or two it was supposed to be free from phylloxera, but the ravages of the fly are now plainly marked. It is intended to replant with resistant vines as rapidly as the old vines die out, and to add one half to the acreage of the vineyard soon by planting resistant vines.

*Faithful, Charles, El Verano.*—Total, 5 acres; table grapes; light gravelly soil; lowland; southern exposure; young vines, no crop being reported.

*Fischer, George, Sonoma.*—Total, 10 acres; all in bearing, and all wine grapes; all infested with phylloxera; good for one more crop, 5 acres, and for more than another crop, 5 acres; soil black loam; low lying; southern exposure; crop, 25 tons; stock of wine on hand, 700 gallons; cooperage, 20,000 gallons, all redwood. Mr. Fischer says that he will not plant resistant vines, but as his vines die out will go out of the business.

*Formschlag, John, Penn's Grove.*—Total, 5 acres; all wine grapes, and all in bearing; soil gravelly loam; upland; southeast exposure; crop, 7 tons; makes a little wine and sells to his neighbors; has about 300 gallons on hand.

*Fridiger, Jacob, Glen Ellen.*—Total, 15 acres; all in bearing, and all wine grapes; light ashy soil; mountain; southern exposure; crop, 30 tons.

*Fritz, John, Petaluma.*—Total, 45 acres; all in bearing, and all wine grapes; soil gravelly loam and deep black loam; upland, rolling hills; principally southwestern exposure; crop, 145 tons.
This vineyard was planted and has been cared for by a Mr. Johnson, who has given the place superior attention. The vines have made a splendid growth and are looking well, except one spot two rods square, which has every appearance of being infested by phylloxera.

*Gatey, Mrs., Glen Ellen.*—Total, 15 acres; all wine grapes and the vines have just come into bearing; infested by phylloxera, 5 acres, all good for more than another crop; planted to resistants (Riparia), 10 acres, all of which are grafted and in bearing; soil red loam; mountain; south and west exposure; crop, 20 tons.

*Glaister, T. S., Sonoma.*—Total, 150 acres; all wine grapes, 100 acres being in bearing; infested by phylloxera, 50 acres; good for one more crop, 30 acres; good for more than another crop, 20 acres; planted to resistants, 100 acres, of which 2 acres are Riparia and 96 acres Lenoir, the other 2 acres being in other varieties; the Elvira reported as doing well; Semillon and other varieties grafted on Lenoir have made good growth; grafted and in bearing, 60 acres; grafted and not in bearing, 40 acres; soil, part black loam, part light sandy, and part stiff adobe; upland; greater portion of the vineyard almost level, other portions rolling in all directions; in some blocks took out all the vines and replanted throughout with resistants, in other renewed as the old vines died; crop, 30,000 gallons; stock of wine on hand, 18,000 gallons; cooperage, 60,000 gallons, half being oak and half redwood.
Mr. Glaister considers the Tokay an excellent resistant vine. He grafted Zinfandels on Tokay roots eighteen years ago and the vines are still alive and giving good returns, while vines all about them have died. The large rootage of the Tokays in autumn makes them strong to resist attacks of phylloxera. He cut Malvoisie eight inches below the surface and grafted with Lenoir. They made a great growth and the second year he put in Semillon and the next year had a full crop. His resistants have made best growth on stiff adobe soil.

*Goldstein, Wm., "Mt. Pisgah Vineyard," Sonoma.*—Total, 200 acres: all in wine grapes; 100 acres bearing; infested by phylloxera, 180 acres; good for one more crop, about 100 acres; soil red loam; mountain; southern exposure; has not given the infested vines any special attention, but has dug out as they have ceased to produce; crop, 200 tons; stock of wine on hand, 15,000 gallons; cooperage, 20,000 gallons, of which 3,000 is oak and 17,000 gallons is redwood. This vineyard is on very fine soil for wine grapes, and made a fine record until attacked by phylloxera.

*Gundlach, J., Sonoma.*—Total, 150 acres; all wine grapes; 140 acres in bearing; all resistant vines—Riparia, 10 acres; Lenoir, 50 acres, while many other varieties are represented; grafted and in bearing, 140 acres; grafted and not in bearing, 10 acres; soil, part gravel and part clay loam; upland; greater portion of vineyard almost level; changed as old vines died and planted resistants; crop, about 220 tons; stock of wine on hand, about 20,000 gallons; cooperage, 90,000 gallons, 35,000 gallons being of oak and 55,000 gallons of redwood. Mostly white wines are made on this place.

*Goodman, W. C., Sonoma.*—Total, 18 acres; all bearing and all in wine grapes; soil black loam; low lying; southwest exposure; crop, 80 tons.

*Gough, M. G., Sonoma.*—Total, 30 acres; all wine grapes; 20 acres in bearing; good for one more crop, 10 acres; good for more than another crop, 10 acres; planted to resistants, 10 acres—Lenoir, 5 acres; other varieties, 5 acres; grafted and in bearing, 5 acres; not yet grafted, 5 acres; soil adobe; low lying; crop, not reported, but estimated at 20 tons. Expects to take out all his vines not resistant next year and try some other crop awhile.

*Graham, A. D., El Verano.*—Total, 5 acres; table grapes; soil light gravel; low lying; southern exposure; crop, none, the vines being too young to produce.

*Groeskopf, A., Glen Ellen.*—Total, 25 acres; in bearing, 15 acres; all wine grapes; all infested by phylloxera; good for more than another crop, 15 acres; soil light gravel; mountain; south and east exposure; crop, 30 tons. There is a small wine cellar on the place, but the cooperage is not large and there is no wine on hand.

*Hall, Robert, Sonoma.*—Total, 45 acres; wine grapes, 42 acres; table grapes, 3 acres; sediment land, 20 feet to gravel; low lying, along the bank of Sonoma Creek; level land; crop, 274 tons.

*Halstead, Robert, Agua Caliente.*—Total, 20 acres; in bearing, 12 acres; in wine grapes, 12 acres; in table grapes, 8 acres; infested by phylloxera, 12 acres, all good for more than another crop; soil light loam; low lying; southern exposure; crop, 35 tons.

*Hansen, G., Sonoma.*—Total, 15 acres, all in bearing and all wine grapes; all infested by phylloxera, and good for more than another crop; planted to resistants, 12 acres (Lenoir), the resistants being set out by the side of the old vines, and all growing well; crop, 15 tons.

*Hardin, H. A., Lakeville.*—Total, 18 acres; in bearing, 16 acres; wine grapes, 15 acres; table grapes, 3 acres; soil part loam and part mixed with adobe; upland; western exposure; crop, about 20 tons.

*Harper, John, Sonoma.*—Total, 15 acres; all in bearing; wine grapes, 10 acres; table grapes, 5 acres; infested by phylloxera, 4 acres; planted to resistants, 2 acres (Riparia); grafted and in bearing, 2 acres; soil gravelly loam; upland; southern exposure; crop, estimated at 9 tons.

*Harris, G. C., Sonoma.*—Total, 15 acres; in wine grapes, 5 acres; in table grapes, 10 acres; in bearing, 0 acres; soil black loam; low lying; exposure west; crop, 25 tons.

*Haubert, A. J., "Bella Vista," San Luis.*—Total, 45 acres; all in wine grapes; in bearing, 30 acres; soil light gravelly; upland; southern exposure; crop, 65 tons.

*Hearst (estate of), "Madrone Vineyard," Agua Caliente.*—Total, 350 acres; all in wine grapes; in bearing, 150 acres; soil light gravelly and red soil; upland and valley; southern exposure; crop, 150 tons.
There is a large wine cellar and distillery connected with this vineyard. The vines are of choice varieties; all grafted upon resistant stocks since the destruction of the old vineyard by phylloxera.

*Heggie, N. J., Agua Caliente.*—Total, 12 acres; in wine grapes, 10 acres; in table grapes, 2 acres; soil black loam; valley; northern exposure; crop, 12 tons.

*Helbery, F., Shellville.*—Total, 5 acres; in wine grapes; in bearing, 1 acre; crop, 4 tons.

*Heller, M. (estate of), Sonoma.*—Total, 100 acres; in wine grapes; in bearing, 15 acres; soil red gravelly loam, generally some black loam; upland; exposure slightly rolling and west slopes; crop, 23 tons; cooperage, oak, 6,000 gallons; redwood, 6,000 gallons. Has a few table grapes that do as well on Riparia as do wine grapes.

*Hendley, John M., Glen Ellen.*—Total, 10 acres; all in bearing; soil red gravelly; mountain; southern exposure; crop, 24 tons.

*Hilton, William H., Glen Ellen.*—Total, 21 acres; in bearing, 3 acres; soil part rocky, part clayey, and part loamy; part low lying and part hill land; exposure in all directions; no crop, all the old vines being dead from phylloxera. Californica considered not resistant. Planted some Cabernet Sauvignon, but it is too shy a bearer to pay. Considers the Zinfandel good enough for a red wine when properly made and handled. Has some that has been pronounced by experts "a fine wine."

*Hodge, Robert, Los Guilicos.*—Total, 10 acres; all in bearing; soil dark loam; valley; southern exposure; crop, 36 tons.

*Hooper, Colonel George F., "Sobre Vista," Agua Caliente.*—Total, 100 acres; in wine grapes, 75 acres; in table grapes, 25 acres; soil red and black gravelly; mountain; northern exposure; crop, 130 tons.
This is one of the oldest and best known vineyards of the Sonoma Valley, the reputation of its wines being world-wide. The vineyard is of choice varieties, and situated on the northern base of the Sonoma Mountain. Phylloxera seems to have made no appearance in the upland or mountain portion.

*Howe, Robert, "Eden Dale," Sonoma.*—Total, 50 acres; in wine grapes, 20 acres; in table grapes, 30 acres.
Mr. Howe says: "All my new vines are Tokay; they appear to resist the phylloxera; have not planted any resistant vines, as life is too short to wait for them to bear a crop."

*Hurd, Rudolph, Glen Ellen.*—Total, 10 acres; all in bearing; soil red gravelly; mountain; southern exposure; a young vineyard, but will bear this year.

*Hyde, W., Sonoma.*—Total, 180 acres; in wine grapes; in bearing, 90 acres; soil light gravelly; upland; southern exposure; when vines found attacked, planted resistant between rows and took out old vines as they died out; crop, 150 tons; wine on hand, 20,000 gallons; cooperage, oak, 3,000 gallons; redwood, 25,000 gallons.
Mr. Hyde has a fine place on the north side of Sonoma Valley. The whole place was planted to old vines, which have been dying for several years, but by planting resistants between the rows the vineyard has been kept in bearing.

*Jones & Winfield, San Francisco* (vineyard near Glen Ellen).—Total, 30 acres; all in bearing; soil light gravelly; mountain; southern exposure; crop, 13 tons.
This vineyard is less than half its former size, phylloxera having played havoc with the greater portion of it.

*Jordan, John, Petaluma.*—Total, 80 acres; all in bearing; soil light loam; mountain; crop, 150 tons.
This vineyard is on Sonoma Mountain. No phylloxera was found in this or neighboring vineyards.

*Kennedy, C. A., Glen Ellen.*—Total, 12 acres; all in bearing; soil red; upland; southern exposure; crop, 30 tons.

*Kearney, Mrs. E., El Verano.*—Total, 8 acres; all in bearing; soil red; upland; southern exposure; crop, 15 tons.

*Keenan, Andrew, Lakeville.*—Total, 20 acres; all in bearing; soil red and abobc; upland; southwest exposure; crop, 65 tons.

*Knight, L., Glen Ellen.*—Total, 20 acres; in wine grapes, 15 acres; in table grapes, 5 acres; soil light loam; valley; northern exposure; crop, 30 tons.
Originally a 40-acre vineyard, but it is being rapidly killed by phylloxera.

*Kohler & Frohling, Glen Ellen.*—Total, 125 acres; in wine grapes; in bearing, 70 acres; soil light gravelly; mountain; northern exposure; crop, 70 tons; cooperage, oak, 50,000 gallons; redwood, 300,000 gallons.
This place is finely situated at the northern base of Sonoma Mountain, and formerly consisted of about 200 acres in vines—all killed by phylloxera and reset to resistant vines. There is a large wine cellar and distillery.

*La Motte, A. V., Glen Ellen.*—Total, 35 acres; in wine grapes; in bearing, 23 acres; soil light gravelly; valley and hill; northern and western exposure; when the vines have been attacked, they have been taken out and the ground set to resistant vines; crop, 35 tons.

*Lang, Mrs. K., Sonoma.*—Total, 8 acres; all in bearing; soil light ashy; valley; northern exposure; crop, 7 tons.

*Leeding, C. F., Sonoma.*—Total, 20 acres; in bearing, 7 acres; in wine grapes, 6 acres; in table grapes, 1 acre; soil gravelly loam; valley; when phylloxera showed, dug up the vines; crop, 30 tons.

*Loumbos, John, Sonoma.*—Total, 15 acres; in wine grapes; soil red gravelly; valley; northern exposure; crop, all young vines.
Place all reset to resistant vines; a small cellar and distillery.

*Lubeck, Mrs. A., Sonoma.*—Total, 14 acres; all in bearing; soil black loam; valley; southern exposure; crop, 18 tons.

*Luderman, Carl, Sonoma.*—Total, 5 acres; all in bearing; soil light gravelly; valley; southern exposure; crop, 5 tons.

*Madison, J. II., Sonoma.*—Total, 30 acres; in wine grapes. 15 acres; in table grapes, 15 acres; soil loose red; upland; southwest exposure; crop, 50 tons. East of Sonoma, on hills.

*Marti, M., Sonoma.*—Total, 20 acres; all in bearing; soil black loam; valley; southern exposure; crop, 20 tons.

*Martini, D., Sonoma.*—Total, 14 acres; all in bearing; soil light gravelly; valley; southern exposure; crop, 3 tons; all young vines, just beginning to bear.

*McGinty, James, Glen Ellen.*—Total, 10 acres; all in bearing; soil gravelly loam; mountain; southern exposure; crop, 20 tons.

*Mills, Mrs. II., Lakeville.*—Total, 15 acres; all in bearing; soil adobe and heavy red loam; low lying; northwest exposure; crop, 42 tons.

*Monahan, P., Glen Ellen.*—Total, 10 acres; in wine grapes; in bearing, 2 acres; soil gravelly; mountain; northern exposure; crop, 2 tons.

*Morris Brothers, Agua Caliente.*—Total, 30 acres; in wine grapes, 20 acres; in table grapes, 10 acres; soil black loam; valley; southern and westerly exposure; crop, 65 tons. Rich valley land. As fast as vines die from phylloxera they replant with resistants.

*Morton, M. T., Sonoma.*—Total, 10 acres; in wine grapes, 9 acres; in table grapes, 1 acre; in bearing, 6 acres; soil black loam; valley; southern exposure; crop, 50 tons.

*Moser, Otto, Sonoma.*—Total, 5 acres; in wine grapes, 3 acres; in table grapes, 2 acres; soil light loam; valley; southern exposure; no crop, the vines being too young to bear.

*Norris, Shubrick, Sonoma.*—Total, 31 acres; in bearing, 28 acres; in wine grapes, 28 acres; in table grapes, 3 acres; soil light loam; valley; southern exposure; has dug up infested vines as soon as discovered; crop, 65 tons.

*O'Brien, John, Sonoma.*—Total, 10 acres; all in bearing; soil red; upland; northern exposure; crop, 20 tons.

*Orsi, R., Sonoma.*—Total, 14 acres; in wine grapes; in bearing, 6 acres; soil light loam; valley; southern exposure; crop, 2 tons, lost by frost.

*Osborne, Mrs., Glen Ellen.*—Total, 5 acres; all in bearing; soil light red gravelly; mountain; eastern exposure; crop, 2 tons.

*Pacific Improvement Company, El Verano.*—Total, 28 acres; in wine grapes; in bearing, 12 acres; soil adobe, sandy, and black loam; valley; northern exposure; crop, 72 tons; wine on hand, 7,000 gallons; cooperage, 10,000 gallons. Much of this vineyard has been trained to trellises.

*Peter, Martin, Glen Ellen.*—Total, 35 acres; in wine grapes; in bearing, 10 acres; soil red; mountain; eastern exposure; crop, 26 tons; wine on hand, 10,000 gallons; cooperage, oak, 40,000 gallons; redwood, 10,000 gallons.

*Peters, I. K., Sonoma.*—Total, 10 acres; all in bearing; soil light loam; valley; southern exposure; crop, 15 tons.

*Pilastre & Gouail, El Verano.*—Total, 8 acres; in wine grapes, 2 acres; in table grapes, 6 acres; soil light gravel; valley; southern exposure; all young vines, and therefore no crop.

*Poppe, J. A., Sonoma.*—Total, 16 acres; all in bearing; soil loam; valley; eastern exposure; as vines have been attacked, they have been taken out and resistants planted; crop, 20 tons; wine on hand, 6,000 gallons; cooperage, oak, 10,000 gallons; redwood, 5,000 gallons.

*Prunty, L. C., Sonoma.*—Total, 45 acres; in wine grapes, 44 acres; in table grapes, 1 acre; soil black and light sandy loam; low lying; exposure direct for both sun and wind; crop, 100 tons.
Mr. Prunty says: "I have only been three years handling vineyard. Phylloxera has appeared in spots. By using a sub-irrigation with a solution of copperas water it has a beneficial effect, though I am transplanting with French prunes."

*Proletti, G., Sonoma.*—Total, 7 acres; in wine grapes; in bearing, 3 acres; soil light gravelly loam; upland; exposure, slightly rolling in most directions; crop, 1¼ tons; wine on hand, 250 gallons; cooperage, oak, 4,000 gallons; redwood, 4,000 gallons.

*Ringstrom, S. A., Sonoma.*—Total, 12 acres; all in bearing; soil light gravelly; upland; western exposure; crop, 10 tons.

*Rogers, W. K., Sonoma.*—Total, 35 acres; all in bearing; soil gravelly loam; upland; crop, 70 tons.
Mr. Rogers says: "I had 150 acres of Mission and Zinfandel, all of which were killed by phylloxera. I then planted 35 acres of Zinfandel up in the hills, which vineyard has now run several years without being affected by anything."

*Rufus, Mrs. F., Sonoma.*—Total, 26 acres; in wine grapes; in bearing, 15 acres; soil black loam; upland; all sick vines have been dug up; crop, 40 tons.
Mrs. Rufus says: "Our drawback in this district has been the low price of grapes (wine), which has had the effect to practically stop the planting of resistant vines, leaving the land bare or planted to fruit trees, much to be regretted by wine men."

*Savings Bank of Santa Rosa (the old "Watson Place"), Santa Rosa.*—Total, 30 acres; in wine grapes; in bearing, 25 acres; soil red gravelly; mountain; west and south exposure; crop, 30 tons.
This vineyard is situated on mountains north of Glen Ellen. Once a much larger vineyard, but now greatly reduced in size by phylloxera.

*Savings Bank of Santa Rosa, Santa Rosa.*—Total, 50 acres; in wine grapes, 6 acres; in bearing, 6 acres; soil red; mountain; exposure direct to both sun and wind; crop, 15 tons.

*Scheick, Gottfried, Glen Ellen.*—Total, 20 acres; in wine grapes; in bearing, 5 acres; soil adobe; mountain; northern exposure; young vineyard, coming into bearing.
The old vineyard is all dead; the new vineyard of resistant vines was set out on new land. Situated at northern base of Sonoma Mountain.

*Schwartz, Henry, and Pacific Bank, Los Guilicos.*—Total, 40 acres; all in bearing; soil mixed; mountain; west and south exposure; crop, 26 tons.

*Seipp, J. C., Sonoma.*—Total, 20 acres; in wine grapes; in bearing, 10 acres; soil mostly heavy; low lying; full exposure.

*Shaw, Jas. A., Kenwood.*—Total, 100 acres; in wine grapes, 90 acres; in table grapes, 10 acres; in bearing, 75 acres; soil red and black loam; hill and valley; southern exposure; diseased vines taken out and resistants planted; crop, 60 tons; wine on hand, 100,000 gallons; cooperage, oak, 100,000 gallons.
Resistants from four to seven years old show no signs of phylloxera. A fine vineyard on red hill land, on north side of valley between Los Guilicos and Glen Ellen. Has planted fruit trees in the valley vineyard between vines.

*Shaw, O. B., Sonoma.*—Total, 12 acres; in wine grapes, 7 acres; in table grapes, 5 acres; in bearing, 7 acres; soil light loam; valley; southern exposure; crop, 20 tons.

*Sheds, Peter, Sonoma.*—Total, 10 acres; in wine grapes; soil light gravelly; mountain; north and east exposure; no crop; young vines that will begin bearing this year.

*Steadler, J. G., Petaluma.*—Total, 18 acres; all in bearing; soil gravelly loam; upland; southeast exposure; crop, 22 tons; one third of the crop lost; wine on hand, 2,000 gallons; cooperage, oak, 2,000 gallons; redwood, 3,000 gallons.

*Sonoma Valley Bank, Sonoma.*—Total, 43 acres; in wine grapes; soil light loam; southern exposure; young vines, not yet in bearing.

*Steiger, Edward, "Johannisburg," Agua Caliente.*—Total, 15 acres; in wine grapes, 10 acres; in table grapes, 5 acres; in bearing, 2 acres; soil red loam; upland and mountain; exposure, none; crop, 2 tons; wine on hand, 600 gallons; cooperage, oak, 12,000 gallons; redwood, 8,000 gallons.

*Stevenot, E. K., Sonoma.*—Total, 30 acres; in wine grapes, 5 acres; in table grapes, 25 acres; in bearing, 5 acres; soil light loam; low lying; south exposure; crop, 3 tons.

*Stein, G., Glen Ellen.*—Total, 15 acres; in wine grapes; in bearing, 10 acres; soil red gravelly; mountain; southern exposure; crop, 20 tons; wine on hand, 5,000 gallons; cooperage, redwood, 5,000 gallons.

This vineyard is near the top of the Sonoma and Napa range of mountains; is infested with phylloxera; about one third destroyed; no resistants planted.

*Tarrant, S. A., Glen Ellen.*—Total, 25 acres; in bearing, 20 acres; soil rich bottom land, good drainage; some upland; southeast exposure; crop, 45 tons. Is rather inclined to let the vineyard die out, and plant "something that will pay," as Mr. Tarrant says.

*Terry, Mrs. B., Sonoma.*—Total, 30 acres; in bearing, 12 acres; in wine grapes, 27 acres; in table grapes, 3 acres; soil light gravelly; valley; southern exposure; crop, 20 tons.

*Todd, J. M., Petaluma.*—Total, 10 acres; in wine grapes, 8 acres; in table grapes, 2 acres; soil red, mostly; mountain; south and west exposure; crop, 22 tons.

Mr. Todd says: "There is no phylloxera on this mountain, as far as I know, at present. The Zinfandel have produced a very fair crop the last three years, and the vines are in a healthy condition; have 2½ acres of old Mission vines twenty-seven years old, which bear a good crop every year. My red and white Chasselas are good bearers."

*Thompson, W. A., Glen Ellen.*—Total, 8 acres; all bear this year; soil black gravelly loam; upland; north and east exposure; when found affected by disease vines have been dug up and thrown away; wine on hand, 18,000 gallons; cooperage, oak, 15,000 gallons; redwood, 10,000 gallons. The old vineyard was first attacked about six years ago, and was destroyed in about three years.

*Thompson, William, Sonoma.*—Total, 25 acres; all in bearing; soil varied—adobe and black loam; upland; south exposure; crop, 8 tons.

Old vineyard began dying about five years ago; all gone last year. Uses the whip or splice grafts, putting them into resistants level with ground; fills dirt around and uses nothing else to hold the parts together.

*Vollman, George, Sonoma.*—Total, 18 acres; in wine grapes, 10 acres; in table grapes, 8 acres; soil gravelly loam; low lying; southern exposure; crop, 20 tons; wine on hand, 4,000 gallons; cooperage, 4,000 gallons.

*Ward, Captain, Los Guilicos.*—Total, 5 acres; in wine grapes; soil red; mountain; southern exposure; young vines, not yet in bearing.

*Wadsworth, John, Sonoma.*—Total, 9 acres; in wine grapes; in bearing, 4 acres; soil gravelly; low lying; when affected, grubbed vines up and burnt them; crop, 6 tons.

*Watress, F., Agua Caliente.*—Total, 20 acres; in wine grapes; in bearing, 10 acres; soil light red; valley; southern exposure; crop, 30 tons; cooperage, oak, 15,000 gallons; redwood, 10,000 gallons.

Mr. Watress says: "Some of my vines have died from what is known as the 'Southern Vine Disease,' or symptoms similar." Grafts resistant vines as near surface as possible.

*Weaver, A. J., Glen Ellen.*—Total, 7 acres; in wine grapes, 6 acres; in table grapes, 1 acre; soil mixed sand and clay; upland; eastern exposure; when disease affects vines, digs them out and plants grain in their stead; crop, 40 tons. Has dug up more than half the vines the past winter.

*Walls, David, Sonoma.*—Total, 10 acres; all in bearing; soil loam; crop, 15 tons.

*Wegener, Joseph, Glen Ellen.*—Total, 10 acres; in bearing, 2 acres; soil loamy volcanic red; sidehill mountain; southeast exposure; crop, 1 ton; wine on hand, 2,000 gallons; cooperage, oak, 15,000 gallons; redwood, 15,000 gallons.

The stock of wine on hand made from bought grapes. Probably nothing will be replanted or grafted unless wine prices go higher. At present prices, find it non-paying industry.

*Weise Estate, Glen Ellen.*—Total, 5 acres; all in bearing, soil red gravelly; mountain; south and west exposure; crop, 15 tons. Once a large vineyard, but about destroyed by phylloxera.

*White, J. H., Lakeville.*—Total, 25 acres; in wine grapes, 23 acres; in table grapes, 2 acres; soil gravelly loam; upland; south and southwest exposure; crop, 80 tons.

*Wilson, Chas., Glen Ellen.*—Total, 5 acres; all in bearing; soil light gravelly; valley; southern exposure; crop, 10 tons.

*Winkle, W., San Francisco* (vineyard near Sonoma).—Total, 50 acres; in wine grapes; soil volcanic; low lying; southwest exposure; crop, 28 tons; wine on hand, 12,000 gallons; cooperage, oak, 18,000 gallons.

*Wiswell, N., Petaluma*—Total, 6 acres; all in bearing; soil adobe; low lying; southwest exposure; frost killed last year's crop.

Mr. Wiswell planted his vines ten feet apart each way; he dug a hole a foot square and a foot deep, filling the same with rich sandy loam, in which he planted each vine; the vines have made fine growth.

*Woods, A. S., Glen Ellen.*—Total, 5 acres; all in bearing; soil red; mountain; west and south exposure; crop, 2 tons.

*Yost, Mrs. J. D., Glen Ellen.*—Total, 9 acres; in bearing, 3 acres; in wine grapes, 3 acres; in table grapes, 6 acres; soil red; 3 acres low, 6 acres upland; eastern exposure; when vines attacked, pulled them up; crop, 10 tons.

*Zane, J. M., Glen Ellen.*—Total, 15 acres; in wine grapes; in bearing, 7 acres; soil light gravelly loam; valley and upland; northern exposure; crop, 15 tons. Expects to replant about 10 acres of old vineyard to Riparia next year.

# SECOND DISTRICT.

## COMPRISING ANALY AND PETALUMA TOWNSHIPS.

*Adamson, Mrs. N. J., Penn's Grove.*—Total, 10 acres; all in bearing; soil clay loam; upland; exposure all directions; crop, 60 tons.

*Allen, Otis, Sebastopol.*—Total, 17 acres; in bearing, 10 acres; in wine grapes, 16 acres; in table grapes, 1 acre; soil red loam, 10 acres; gravel loam, 7 acres; upland; slopes nearly all directions; crop, 22 tons; about one third of crop rotted on the ground; has recently planted 6 acres of Semillon.

*Anderson, L. S., Forestville.*—Total, 5 acres; all in bearing; soil sandy loam; upland; south and west exposure; crop, 20 tons; has planted prunes in the vineyard, and will take up the vines as soon as the trees are in bearing.

*Ayer, H. G., Sebastopol.*—Total, 13 acres; all in bearing; soil sandy loam; upland; western exposure; crop, 46 tons.

*Barnes, Henry, Sebastopol.*—Total, 16 acres; all in bearing; soil sandy loam; upland; western exposure; crop, 40 tons; vines healthy and good bearers.

*Balfour, Guthrie & Co., Sebastopol.*—Total, 25 acres; all in bearing; soil gravelly, with clay subsoil; upland; southeast exposure; crop, 50 tons.

*Beattie, A., Sebastopol.*—Total, 6 acres; all in bearing; soil light and sandy; mountain; southern exposure; crop, 25 tons.

*Bellman, M., Trenton.*—Total, 10 acres; all in bearing; soil sandy loam; upland; southwest exposure; crop, 18 tons; vineyard located near Forestville.

*Bennett, T. N., Sebastopol.*—Total, 8 acres; all in bearing; soil sandy loam and clay; upland; easterly exposure; crop, 40 tons.

*Bernard, Mr., Petaluma.*—Total, 20 acres; all in bearing; soil gravel loam; upland; exposure all directions; no crop.
This vineyard is located near Trenton, in one of the best vineyard districts of the county, but the owner does not live there, and the place does not receive attention and gives no returns.

*Billings, J. F., Sebastopol.*—Total, 10 acres; all in bearing; soil sandy loam; upland; south and west exposure; crop, 12 tons. The vineyard produced a good crop, but much of it was not saved.

*Bonnardel, P., Sebastopol.*—Total, 20 acres; all in bearing; soil sandy loam; upland; southern exposure; crop, 75 tons.
The property adjoins the town of Sebastopol on the north, and is a heavy bearing and healthy vineyard. There is a small wine cellar, but no wine on hand.

*Briggs, Alfred, Sebastopol.*—Total, 15 acres; in wine grapes, 14 acres; in table grapes, 1 acre; soil sandy loam; upland; eastern exposure; crop, 45 tons.

*Brown, C., Stony Point.*—Total, 30 acres; all in bearing; soil sandy loam; upland; exposure, sloping to the east and south; crop, 90 tons.

*Brown, John, Sebastopol.*—Total, 20 acres; all in bearing; soil sandy loam; upland; southern exposure; crop, 50 tons.

*Bruner, J. W., Sebastopol.*—Total, 10 acres; all in bearing; soil sandy loam; upland; southern exposure; crop, 20 tons.

*Bushnell, A., Forestville.*—Total, 12 acres; all in bearing; soil sandy loam; upland; southwest exposure; crop, 40 tons.
Mr. Bushnell has taken out 3 acres this season, and thinks of digging up more vines, because the crop is not profitable.

*Calder, S. A., Sebastopol.*—Total, 25 acres; all in bearing; soil light sandy loam; upland; eastern exposure; crop, 70 tons.
This vineyard is just south of Sebastopol; has taken out 15 acres of vines, because of their not being profitable.

*Casassa, M., Forestville.*—Total, 10 acres; all in bearing; soil gravelly loam; mountain; exposure, south slope; crop, 20 tons.

*Cesaris, C., Trenton.*—Total, 40 acres; all in bearing; soil sandy loam; upland; east and west exposure; crop, 80 tons; cooperage, redwood, 6,000 gallons.

*Clark & Gamble, Trenton.*—Total, 43 acres; all in bearing; soil sandy loam; upland; exposure, all directions; crop, 100 tons.

*Cody, M., Sebastopol.*—Total, 26 acres; in wine grapes, 18 acres; in table grapes, 8 acres; soil sandy loam; upland; exposure, all directions; crop estimated at 80 tons.

*Compton, T. J., Sebastopol.*—Total, 20 acres; all in bearing; soil sandy loam; upland; southerly exposure; crop, 70 tons.

*Corbin, T. B., Sebastopol.*—Total, 8 acres; in wine grapes, 7½ acres; in table grapes, ½ acre; soil sandy loam; low, lying on west bank of Laguna; easterly exposure; crop, 30 tons; dried about 12 tons.

*Crawford, T., Sebastopol.*—Total, 10 acres; in wine grapes, 8 acres; in table grapes, 2 acres; soil sandy loam; upland; western exposure; crop, 25 tons.

*Dale, Mrs. M., Sebastopol.*—Total, 10 acres; all in bearing; soil sandy loam; upland; northern exposure; crop, 30 tons.

*Davis, Manuel, Sebastopol.*—Total, 18 acres; in wine grapes; in bearing, 10 acres; soil light gravelly; upland; northeast exposure; crop, 30 tons.

*Dietrick, G., Sebastopol.*—Total, 25 acres; in wine grapes; in bearing, 16 acres; soil light gravelly; upland; eastern exposure; crop, 40 tons; grafted on St. Macaire and White Semillon, about 9 acres; situated south of Sebastopol; a small wine cellar.

*Drosbach, C., Sebastopol.*—Total, 6 acres; all in bearing; soil gravelly and red loam; upland; southeasterly exposure; crop, 17 tons; vineyard has been planted six years and is in fine condition.

*Doyle, M. J., Trenton.*—Total, 10 acres; all in bearing; soil sandy loam; upland; eastern exposure; crop, very light; blossoms destroyed by peculiar rain.
This is part of the Cnopius place; all the other vines on the place have been dug up as unprofitable, and the ground devoted to other purposes.

*Ecklemayer, F., Trenton.*—Total, 8 acres; all in bearing; soil sandy and gravelly loam; upland; southern exposure; crop, 25 tons.

*Emerson, J. W., Sebastopol.*—Total, 5 acres; all in bearing; soil sandy loam; upland; southern exposure; crop, 15 tons.

*Evans, E. R., Forestville.*—Total, 30 acres; all in bearing; soil sandy loam; upland; east and south exposure; crop, 170 tons.

*Fine, A. (estate of), Sebastopol.*—Total, 20 acres; in wine grapes, 18 acres; in table grapes, 2 acres; soil sandy, gravelly loam; upland; east and north exposure; crop, 60 tons.

*Fleming, James M., Trenton.*—Total, 20 acres; all in bearing; soil light loam; upland; eastern exposure; crop, 50 tons.

*Fletcher, Mrs. W. R., Forestville.*—Total, 12 acres; all in bearing; soil sandy loam; upland; exposure, all directions; crop, 40 tons.

*Fredericks, George, Sebastopol.*—Total, 35 acres; all in bearing; soil sandy loam; upland; southern exposure; crop, 75 tons.

*Frei, A., Sebastopol.*—Total, 50 acres; all in bearing; soil gravelly loam; upland; western exposure; crop, 80 tons; a stockholder in the Fulton Winery, and delivers his grapes there.

*Frank, Fred., Trenton.*—Total, 7 acres; all in bearing; soil sandy loam; upland; eastern exposure; crop, 15 tons.

*Gamble, A., Santa Rosa.*—Total, 10 acres; all in bearing; soil sandy loam; upland; eastern exposure; crop, 15 tons.

*Gilmore, S., Stony Point.*—Total, 11 acres; all in bearing; soil white loam; upland; south and east exposure; crop, 22 tons.

*Glass, Philip, Trenton.*—Total, 23 acres; all in bearing; soil sandy loam and adobe; upland; exposure, all directions; crop, 65 tons; cooperage, oak, 1,000 gallons; redwood, 2,000 gallons.

*Griffith, N. A., Trenton.*—Total, 9 acres; all in bearing; soil sandy loam; upland; eastern exposure; crop, 20 tons; has taken up 15 acres, and will remove the balance when trees have grown a few years.

*Grass, Peter, Stony Point.*—Total, 30 acres; in wine grapes; 28 acres bearing; soil gravelly loam, part reddish; upland; south and east exposure; crop, 67 tons; wine on hand, 12,000 gallons; cooperage, oak, 12,000 gallons; redwood, 4,000 gallons.

No disease noticed, not even mildew; very particular in sulphuring; has had twenty-six years' experience, and knows the great value of sulphur, properly applied. People who have not been sulphuring have had mildew.

*Hathaway, E. L., Sebastopol.*—Total, 10 acres; in wine grapes, 9 acres; in table grapes, 1 acre; soil sandy loam; upland; southeast exposure; crop, 14 tons.

*Hall, Dan., Petaluma.*—Total, 30 acres; all in bearing and all wine grapes; sandy loam soil; upland; northern exposure; crop, about 45 tons.

*Hayden, E. W., Sebastopol.*—Total, 25 acres; all in bearing; soil light, sandy, and gravelly loam; upland; southern exposure; crop, 70 tons.

*Hill, William, Trenton.*—Total, 150 acres; all in bearing; soil sandy loam; upland; exposure, all directions; crop, 600 tons; wine on hand, 75,000 gallons; cooperage, oak, 2,250 gallons; redwood, 150,000 gallons; made no wine last year, and winery was leased to Dresel & Co., who made some wine there, but shipped most of the grapes to their Sonoma winery.

*Also,* in another vineyard in the same neighborhood: total, 60 acres; all in bearing; soil sandy loam; upland; east and north exposure; crop, 150 tons.

*Hamilton, G. W., Stony Point.*—Total, 40 acres; all in bearing; soil clay; upland; southern exposure; crop, 125 tons.

*Jewett, George E., Forestville.*—Total, 24 acres; all in bearing; soil sandy loam; upland; southern exposure; rolling east and west; crop, 90 tons; 20 tons lost by rain.

*Jewell, Mrs. R. S., Petaluma.*—Total, 80 acres; all in bearing; soil sandy loam; upland; full exposure; crop, 200 tons; wine on hand, 3,000 gallons; cooperage, oak, 2,000 gallons; redwood, 15,000 gallons. Sells most of her grapes; only made 12,000 gallons of wine last year.

*Jones, Richard and William, Trenton.*—Total, 15 acres; all in bearing; soil gravelly loam; upland; west and south exposure; crop, 50 tons.

*Jones Bros., Trenton.*—Total, 12 acres; all in bearing; soil sandy loam; upland; exposure full in all directions; crop, 21 tons.

*Kauffman, Frank, Sebastopol.*—Total, 6 acres; all in bearing; soil sandy loam; upland; southern exposure; crop, 25 tons.

*Lankamp, Peter, Sebastopol.*—Total, 25 acres; all in bearing; soil sandy loam; upland; southern exposure; crop, 55 tons.

*Leiby, Geo., Sebastopol.*—Total, 15 acres; all in bearing; soil sandy loam; upland; southern exposure; crop, 30 tons.

*Leipe, Louis, Sebastopol.*—Total, 8 acres; all in bearing; soil sandy loam; upland; exposure, slopes slightly to the north; crop, 12 tons; cooperage, oak, 1,600 gallons.

*Litchfield, David, Sebastopol.*—Total, 21 acres; in wine grapes, 20 acres; in table grapes, 1 acre; soil gravelly and sandy loam; upland; southern exposure; crop, 60 tons.

*Loftus, P., Stony Point.*—Total, 12 acres; all in bearing; soil loam; upland; easterly exposure; crop, 20 tons.

*Lynch, D. B., Sebastopol.*—Total, 13 acres; in wine grapes, 11 acres; in table grapes, 2 acres; soil yellow clay subsoil; southeastern exposure; crop, 26 tons.

*Lynch, H. A., heirs of, Trenton.*—Total, 21 acres; all in bearing; soil sandy loam; upland; exposure, rolling, slopes in all directions; crop, 30 tons; much of the crop destroyed by late rain.

*Maddock, L., Forestville.*—Total, 10 acres; all in bearing; soil sandy loam; upland; southern exposure; crop, 30 tons.

*Maddock, Lute A., Forestville.*—Total, 5 acres; all in bearing; soil gravelly loam; upland; exposure, slopes south; crop, good last year.

*McClelland, F. S., Trenton.*—Total, 19 acres; all in bearing; soil sandy loam; upland; southerly exposure; crop, 40 tons.

*Mills, E. H., Sebastopol.*—Total, 8 acres; all in bearing; soil sandy loam; upland; southern exposure; crop, 20 tons.

*Mole, J., Sebastopol.*—Total, 12 acres; in wine grapes; in bearing, 11 acres; soil sandy loam; upland; northern and western exposure; crop, 50 tons.

*Morse, W. P. & Son, Sebastopol.*—Total, 10 acres; in wine grapes, 9 acres; in table grapes, 1 acre; soil sandy loam; upland; crop, 32 tons.

*Mugge, Henry, Sebastopol.*—Total, 25 acres; in bearing, 18 acres; soil sandy loam; upland; exposure, easterly slope; crop, 50 tons; wine on hand, 5,000 gallons; cooperage, oak, 2,000 gallons; redwood, 5,000 gallons.

*Murphy, Oscar, Sebastopol.*—Total, 8 acres; all in bearing; soil sandy loam; upland; southern exposure; crop, 15 tons.

Formerly the J. C. Holloway place, and some years ago was a much larger vineyard, but vines have been taken out to give place to fruit trees.

*Murphy, P. H., Stony Point.*—Total, 15 acres; all in bearing; soil sandy and clay loam; upland; exposure, generally eastern; crop, 45 tons.

*Norton, E. A., Forestville.*—Total, 13 acres; all in bearing; soil sandy loam; upland; north and east exposure; crop, 60 tons sold, many spoiled on vines.

*Paddock, E. S., Forestville.*—Total, 27 acres; all in bearing; soil, about half dark sandy loam, balance light, some gravel; upland; south and east exposure; crop, 150 tons.

*Palmer, C. H., Sebastopol.*—Total, 16 acres; all in bearing; soil sandy loam; upland; northern exposure; crop, 40 tons.

*Pelton, J. S., San Francisco.*—Total, 45 acres; in wine grapes, 43 acres; in table grapes, 2 acres; soil sandy loam; upland; exposure, hills sloping nearly all directions; crop, 80 tons saved, considerable lost by rains; cooperage, redwood, 8,000 gallons.

This vineyard is on the Occidental road in the western part of Analy Township. The owner resides in San Francisco, Frank Saviez having charge of the place.

*Pitkin, Levi, Forestville.*—Total, 5 acres; in wine grapes, 3 acres; in table grapes, 2 acres; soil sandy loam; upland; west and south exposure; crop, 13 tons.

*Poole, J. F., Sebastopol.*—Total, 6 acres; in wine grapes, 4 acres; in table grapes, 1 acre; in raisin grapes, 1 acre; soil light sandy loam, clay bottom; upland and hill; crop, 18 tons.

*Ramus, Joseph, Trenton.*—Total, 5 acres; all in bearing; soil sandy loam; upland; south-eastern exposure; crop, 13 tons. The vines on 3 acres have been taken up and the ground planted to fruit trees.

*Ravello, Jos., Trenton.*—Total, 16 acres; all in bearing; soil sandy loam; upland; easterly exposure; crop, 30 tons; many spoiled by rains.

*Raup, William, Sebastopol.*—Total, 10 acres; all in bearing; soil sandy loam; upland; southern exposure; crop, 30 tons.

*Rickard, W. G., Peachland.*—Total, 15 acres; in wine grapes, 14 acres; in table grapes, 1 acre; soil sandy loam; upland; exposure, slight slope to the west and south; crop, 41 tons; has recently grafted an acre of Semillon on other roots.

*Riddle, D. M., Trenton.* Total, 18 acres; all in bearing; soil sandy loam; upland; south and east exposure, slight slope; crop, 34 tons saved; half rotted on account of rains.

*Robertson, James, Forestville.*—Total, 6 acres; all in bearing; soil sandy loam; upland; southwestern exposure; crop, 10 tons.

*Savings Bank of Santa Rosa, Santa Rosa.*—Total, 37 acres; all in bearing; soil gravelly loam and red; upland; exposure,.slopes to the east; crop, 110 tons.

*Schirmer, E., Sebastopol.*—"Belle View Vineyard." Total, 30 acres; all in bearing; soil sandy loam; upland; easterly exposure; crop, 80 tons; wine on hand, 15,000 gallons; cooperage, oak, 20,000 gallons; redwood, 20,000 gallons.

Vineyards in the section above Sebastopol look well and are not affected by any disease; no vines dead; promise of a good crop.

*Shepherd, L. V., Forestville.*—Total, 9 acres; all in bearing; soil sandy and gravelly loam; upland; exposure, part north and part south; crop, 16 tons.

On account of the grape crop not being profitable, 7 acres of this vineyard were dug up, and the ground has been planted to prunes and other fruits.

*Showalter, W., Sebastopol.*—Total, 5 acres; all in bearing; soil light loam; valley; southern exposure; crop, 15 tons.

*Surryhne, E., Trenton.*—Total, 45 acres; all in bearing; soil, 28 acres sandy loam and 17 acres gravelly; upland; exposure, principally southern; crop, 83 tons; made 5,000 gallons of wine, all of which has been sold and delivered; cooperage, oak, 1,000 gallons; redwood, 15,000 gallons.

*Thomas, I., Peachland.*—Total, 10 acres; all in bearing; soil sandy loam; upland; exposure, generally west; crop, 25 tons.

*Tucker, J. S., Sebastopol.*—Total, 20 acres; all in bearing; soil loam; upland; eastern exposure; crop, 40 tons.

*Urton, W. L., Sebastopol.*—Total, 32 acres; in wine grapes, 30 acres; in table grapes' 2 acres; soil sand, clay, and gravel, with subsoil of same; upland; south and east exposure; crop, near 40 tons, without any cultivation whatever.

*Wall, Mr.*—Lives in Lake County, vineyard near Petaluma. Total, 7 acres; all in bearing, and all wine grapes; soil gravelly loam; upland; eastern exposure; crop, estimated at 15 tons.

*Walsh, M., Forestville.*—Total, 15 acres; all in bearing; soil sandy loam; upland; southwest exposure; crop, 60 tons; not all picked.

*Ward, T. M., Peachland.*—Total, 6 acres; all in bearing; soil sandy loam; upland; exposure, west slope; crop, 16 tons.
This vineyard is thirty-four years old, and is perfectly healthy. It is planted to Missions.

*Warner, J. L., Sebastopol.*—Total, 6 acres; all in bearing; soil sandy loam; upland; east and south exposure; crop, 8 tons.

*Weeks, Percy, Sebastopol.*—Total, 20 acres; in wine grapes, 17 acres; in table grapes, 3 acres; soil light sandy and gravelly loam; upland; exposure, all directions; crop, 23 tons; many young vines, bearing last year for first time.

*Whaley, Samuel, Sebastopol.*—Total, 28 acres; in wine grapes, 24 grapes; in table grapes, 4 acres; soil sandy; upland; easterly exposure; crop, 90 tons.
This vineyard affected by black knot, believed to be caused by imperfect cultivation.

*Whiley, Mrs. John W., Peachland.*—Total, 18 acres; all in bearing; soil sandy loam; upland; exposure, slopes all directions, generally south; crop, 40 tons saved, about 15 tons spoiled.

# THIRD DISTRICT.

## COMPRISING SANTA ROSA AND RUSSIAN RIVER TOWNSHIPS.

*Adler, Robert, Windsor.*—Total, 17 acres; in wine grapes, 16 acres; in table grapes, 1 acre; soil light loam above clay subsoil; upland; crop, 47 tons.

*Ahl, Jacob, Santa Rosa.*—Total, 25 acres; all in bearing; soil adobe and volcanic; upland; eastern exposure; crop, 60 tons.

*Alton, John L., Fulton.*—Total, 50 acres; all in bearing; soil light gravelly; rolling; southern exposure; crop, 80 tons; wine on hand, 1,000 gallons; cellar; cooperage, redwood, 40,000 gallons. A good vineyard and winery; vines well taken care of.

*Anderson, John, Windsor.*—Total, 12 acres; all in bearing; soil light loam; valley; southern exposure; crop, 38 tons.

*Andrews, Herbert, Sebastopol.*—Total, 5 acres; all in bearing; soil gravelly loam; upland; western exposure; crop, 8 tons.

*Arata, B., Windsor.*—Total, 16 acres; in wine grapes; in bearing, 12 acres; soil light loam; low lying; exposure, all directions; crop, 10 tons.

*Arenz, Theodore, Santa Rosa.*—Total, 9 acres; all in bearing; soil light loam; valley; southern exposure; crop, 27 tons.

*Arnold, Judson.*—Total, 15 acres; all in bearing; soil black loam; mountain; southeasterly exposure; crop, 40 tons.

*Arnold, A. W., Santa Rosa.*—Total, 18 acres; all in bearing; soil light loam; upland; exposure, nearly level but slightly rolling; crop, 41 tons.

*Atterbury, William, Santa Rosa.*—Total, 10 acres; all in bearing; soil red; mountain; southwestern exposure; crop, not in bearing; a young vineyard in hills on upper Mark West Creek.

*Austin, Jas. & Sons, Santa Rosa.*—Total, 115 acres; all in bearing; soil red loam, clayey and gravelly; upland; exposure southeast and southwest; crop, 315 tons.

*Bachman, John, Healdsburg.*—Total, 12 acres; in wine grapes, 10 acres; in table grapes, 2 acres; soil red stony; upland; exposure north, south, and west; crop, 30 tons.
Mr. Bachman says: "So far we have not had any sign of phylloxera that we know of. We plow twice, cultivate after each rain, sucker and top the vines, and sulphur for mildew."

*Badger, J. J., Rincon.*—Total, 40 acres; all in bearing; soil gravelly loam; upland, but not very high; southern exposure; crop, 53 tons.

*Badger, J. L., Rincon.*—Total, 40 acres; all in bearing; soil gravelly loam; upland, but not very high; southern exposure; crop, 53 tons.

*Badger, D., Santa Rosa.*—Total, 12 acres; all in bearing; soil gravelly loam; low lying; exposure almost level; crop, 35 tons.

*Bailiff, Santa Rosa.*—Total, 65 acres; in wine grapes; in bearing, 64 acres; soil generally red; rolling upland, some adobe near lowest points; exposure, all directions, with no protection; crop, 192 tons; wine on hand, 22,000 gallons; cooperage, oak, 3,600 gallons; redwood, 22,000 gallons.

*Ballou, Mrs. R. A., Santa Rosa.*—Total, 5 acres; all in bearing; soil black loam, part gravelly; upland; exposure, slopes to the north chiefly; crop, 4 tons.

*Barth, A., Windsor.*—Total, 30 acres; all in bearing; soil light gravelly; valley; exposure southern; crop, 100 tons.

*Barnes, A., Sebastopol.*—The vineyard is on hills east of Windsor. Total, 20 acres; all in bearing; soil red gravelly; mountain; western exposure; crop, 20 tons; young vines.

*Barnes, W. P., Fulton.*—Total, 16 acres; all in bearing; soil light clay; valley; southern exposure; crop, 21 tons.

*Barnes, Ruth (estate of), Santa Rosa.*—Total 21 acres; all in bearing; soil sandy loam; upland; south and west exposure; crop, 40 tons.

*Barnett, G. A., Santa Rosa.*—Total, 8 acres; all in bearing; soil light loam; valley; southern exposure; crop, 15 tons.

*Bartley, George, San Francisco.*—This vineyard is near Fulton. Total, 22 acres; in wine grapes; in bearing, 15 acres; soil light clay; valley; southern exposure; crop, 12 tons.

*Benjamin, A., Santa Rosa.*—Total, 28 acres; all in bearing; soil gravelly loam; upland; exposure east; crop, 53 tons.

*Bertoli, P., Santa Rosa.*—Total, 17 acres; all in bearing; soil red loam; upland; exposure east; crop, 5 tons, but very poor, the fruit being killed by a late frost.

*Bertoli, P., Santa Rosa.*—Total, 20 acres; all in bearing; soil dark red loam; upland; exposure east; crop, 40 tons.

*Bell, Warren, Windsor.*—Total, 8 acres; all in bearing; soil light loam; upland; southern exposure; crop, 13 tons.

*Benson, William, Santa Rosa.*—Total, 82 acres; all in bearing; soil red; low lying; southern exposure; crop, 190 tons.

*Bentel, Gottliel, Santa Rosa.*—Total, 12 acres; all in bearing; soil adobe; upland; exposure east; crop, 20 tons, netting 1,500 gallons of wine; wine on hand, 200 gallons; cooperage, oak, 200 gallons; redwood, 1,000 gallons.

*Bolle, Henry, Santa Rosa.*—Total, 90 acres; in wine grapes; in bearing, 40 acres; soil red gravelly; valley; southern exposure; crop, 100 tons; wine on hand, 50,000 gallons; cooperage, oak, 30,000 gallons; redwood, 20,000 gallons.
This vineyard is situated at the base of Hood Mountain, in Los Guilicos Valley. There is a large stone wine cellar and distillery. For the past three or four years phylloxera has been playing sad havoc with this vineyard. Most of the old vines are gone and the day is not distant when the others will be taken; but Mr. Bolle is a hopeful vineyardist, and he is planting resistant vines. In its time his old vineyard was a fine one, and resistant vines are being grown as rapidly as possible.

*Brush, J. H., Santa Rosa.*—Total, 15 acres; in wine grapes, 13 acres; in table grapes, 2 acres; soil volcanic formation; upland; exposure, south and east; crop, 35 tons; considerable not gathered, on account of mildew and low prices.

*Brown, Fred., Windsor.*—Total, 80 acres; all in bearing; soil sandy and gravelly loam; upland; exposure, all directions; crop, 200 tons.

*Bromfield, S., Healdsburg.*—Total, 20 acres; all in bearing; soil light loam; upland; southern exposure; crop, 60 tons.

*Brooks, William, Windsor.*—Total, 12 acres; all in bearing; soil gravelly loam; upland; exposure, slopes in all directions; crop, 36 tons.

*Bucchi, H., Santa Rosa.*—Total, 12 acres; all in bearing; soil gravelly loam; mountain; southern exposure; crop, 40 tons.

*Bucchi, Mrs., Santa Rosa.*—Total, 8 acres; all in bearing; soil sandy loam and clay; upland; exposure east; crop, 20 tons.

*Buckner, A. R., Santa Rosa.*—Total, 38 acres; in wine grapes; in bearing 30 acres; soil red mountain loam; mountain; exposure, slopes slightly to all points of compass; crop, 40 tons; wine on hand, 5,000 gallons old wine, 9,000 gallons of last year's vintage; cooperage, oak, 2,000 gallons; redwood, 30,000 gallons.

*Buckner, J. E., Santa Rosa.*—Total, 20 acres; in wine grapes; in bearing, 10 acres; soil red mountain loam; mountain; exposure south and east; crop, 20 tons.

*Buckner, Horace, Santa Rosa.*—Total, 10 acres; all in bearing; soil red loam; mountain; slightly southern exposure; crop, 20 tons.

*Burnham, A. & Son, Santa Rosa,*—Total, 30 acres; in wine grapes; in bearing, 25 acres— 5 acres more than last year; soil loam, part gravelly and part clay; upland; exposure north; crop, 157 tons; wine on hand, 30,000 gallons; cooperage, oak, 5,000 gallons; redwood, 70,000 gallons.
This vineyard is on the hills or mountains west of Bennett Valley. The vines are free from disease, and are very prolific. The winery is well managed.

*Bussman, A., Santa Rosa.*—Total, 14 acres; all in bearing; soil clay loam; slightly rolling; exposure, slightly rolling; crop, 32 tons.

*Butler, J. S., America.*—Total, 6 acres; in wine grapes; in bearing, 1 acre; soil black gravelly loam; upland; exposure northwest.

*Butler, S. L., America.*—Total, 7 acres; all in bearing; soil red and black loam; upland; exposure southwest: crop, 9 tons; frost took most of last crop.

*Calhoun, J. W., Windsor.*—Total, 14 acres; in wine grapes; in bearing, 8 acres; soil light gravelly; upland; exposure south and east; crop, 20 tons.

*Cardina, John, Windsor.*—Total, 8 acres; all in bearing; soil light loam; mountain; eastern exposure; crop, 10 tons.

*Carr, Nelson, Santa Rosa.*—Total, 37 acres; all in bearing; soil, 17 acres of light gravelly loam and 20 acres firmer and closer; upland; exposure south; crop, 126 tons.

*Cassassa, D., Santa Rosa.*—Total, 50 acres; all in bearing; soil light clay; valley; southern exposure; crop, 100 tons; a small cellar, having cooperage of about 12,000 gallons.

*Cash, Mrs., Santa Rosa.*—Total, 5 acres; all in bearing; soil light sandy loam; upland; southern exposure; crop, 3 tons.

*Catron, Mrs. E., Santa Rosa.*—Total, 18 acres; all in bearing; soil red loam, principally lying in Chestnut Valley; valley between hills; southern exposure; crop, 18 tons; crop much damaged.

*Chapman, George, Santa Rosa.*—Total, 18 acres; all in bearing; soil black loam; upland; exposure, all directions; crop, 55 tons.

*Chandler, R. O., Santa Rosa.*—Total, 18 acres; in wine grapes, 12 acres; in table grapes, 6 acres; soil black loam; upland; exposure, slightly rolling in all directions; crop, 60 tons.

*Chisolm, John, Windsor.*—Total, 13 acres; all in bearing; soil light gravelly, with clay subsoil; upland; western exposure; crop, 22½ tons. This vineyard is young, last year being the second crop.

*Christianson, Jacob, Healdsburg.*—Total, 7 acres; all in bearing; soil red; valley; southern exposure; crop, 17 tons.

*Clark, Benj., Windsor.*—Total, 7 acres; all in bearing; soil gravelly loam and clay loam; upland; southern exposure; crop, 22 tons.

*Clark, James, "Oakhill," Windsor.*—Total, 18 acres; all in bearing; soil red gravelly; upland; eastern exposure; crop, 54 tons.

*Clark, George, Santa Rosa.*—Total, 50 acres; in wine grapes, 45 acres; in table grapes, 5 acres; soil loam, volcanic; upland; exposure south; crop, 90 tons.

*Clarke, Fred., Santa Rosa.*—Total, 70 acres; all in bearing; soil red gravelly; valley; southern exposure; crop, 90 tons.
A number of vines have died in this vineyard, but it is not known that phylloxera killed them.

*Cooper, Lewis, Santa Rosa.*—Total, 11 acres; all in bearing; soil light gravelly; rolling hill; southern exposure; crop, 22 tons.

*Cooper, heirs of, Windsor.*—Total, 20 acres; all in bearing; soil gravelly; upland; exposure south and east; crop, 40 tons.

*Cook, J. F., Santa Rosa.*—Total, 10 acres; all in bearing; soil gravelly loam; upland; exposure slight; crop, 15 tons.

*Colburn, Chas., Santa Rosa (leased by Liggett).*—Total, 7 acres; all in bearing; soil light sandy loam; upland; exposure, level; crop, 10 tons; light crop, not properly cared for.

*Coulter, S. F., Santa Rosa.*—Total, 12 acres; all in bearing; soil reddish yellow on tufa basis; upland; exposure, all directions except east; crop, 32 tons.

*County Farm of Sonoma, Santa Rosa.*—Total, 23 acres; all in bearing; soil part adobe and part gravelly loam; upland and lowland; exposure, all directions; crop, 54 tons.

*Cowan, William, Santa Rosa.*—Total, 16 acres; all in bearing; soil red loam; upland; exposure south and west; crop, 30 tons.
Phylloxera has been here some five or six years, and has done the vineyard great damage.

*Crane, Robert, Santa Rosa.*—Total, 53 acres; all in bearing; soil gravelly loam, part black loam; upland; 35 acres slope south, balance in all directions; sold 90 tons and about equal amount rotted.
Mr. Crane plows his vineyard three times in spring of year, and cultivates with harrow and hoe.

*Crane, R. H., Santa Rosa.*—Total, 12 acres; all in bearing; soil part red and part black loam; upland; exposure south; crop, 36 tons—about equal amount spoiled by rains.

*Cralle, L. J., Santa Rosa.*—Total, 76 acres; all in bearing; soil red gravelly; valley; southern exposure; crop, 140 tons; cooperage, oak, 5,000 gallons; redwood, 35,000 gallons. Vineyard not in good condition for want of cultivation.

*Crooks, R. L., Santa Rosa.*—Total, 125 acres; in wine grapes; in bearing, 100 acres; soil gravelly loam; upland; exposure, slopes in all directions; crop, 90 tons; frost caught the place last season.

*Cunningham, Z. H. & Son, Windsor.*—Total, 35 acres; all in bearing; soil gravelly; rolling land; exposure south; crop, 65 tons; wine on hand, 3,000 gallons; cooperage, oak, 4,000 gallons; redwood, 6,000 gallons.

*Davis, E. W., Yulupa, via Santa Rosa.*—Total, 80 acres; all in bearing, soil foothill and alluvial; upland; full exposure to sun, protected from north wind; vines, as soon as disease shows, have been pulled out; crop, 300 tons; wine on hand, 40,000 gallons; cooperage, oak, 18,000 gallons; redwood, 132,000 gallons.
The vineyards in this part of Bennett Valley are just beginning to show signs of phylloxera, and owners are uprooting as fast as the disease appears, and are planting trees.

*Davis, George W., Santa Rosa.*—Total, 50 acres; all in bearing; soil red foothill; foothill and rolling; exposure southwest, sheltered from wind; crop, 250 tons; wine on hand, 50 gallons; cooperage, oak, 18,000 gallons; redwood, 92,000 gallons.
The vineyard is at full bearing; cellar in perfect order; place in healthful location.

*Delzell, W. B., Santa Rosa.*—Total, 16 acres; all in bearing; soil loam; upland; exposure, all directions; crop, 22 tons; frost caught one vineyard a year ago.

*Descalso, L., Santa Rosa.*—Total, 6 acres; all in bearing; soil light loam; upland; exposure, nearly level; crop, 6 tons; some 1,500 gallons oak cooperage, purchased second-hand, to be overhauled.

*Detroy, Chas., Santa Rosa.*—Total, 12 acres; all in bearing; soil black loam; upland; southern exposure; crop, very poor, only 9 tons saved.

*Dickinson, J. Read, Windsor.*—Total, 50 acres; in wine grapes, 40 acres; in table grapes, 10 acres; soil sandy loam; rolling; crop, 100 tons; wine on hand, 800 gallons for own use; cooperage, oak, 1,000 gallons; redwood, 6,000 gallons.

*Diandi, D., Santa Rosa.*—Total, 25 acres; all in bearing; soil adobe; low lying; exposure, level; crop, 6 tons; a young vineyard just coming into bearing; wine on hand, 1,000 gallons; cooperage, redwood, 1,000 gallons.

*Dillon, James, Santa Rosa.*—Total, 10 acres; all in bearing; soil sandy loam; upland; exposure, almost level; crop, 30 tons.

*Dixon, John, Santa Rosa.*—Total, 52 acres; in wine grapes; in bearing, 49 acres; soil light colored loam; upland principally; exposure, all directions; declined to state crop, but estimated at 100 tons; declined to state stock of wine on hand; cooperage, oak, 28,000 gallons. Has planted 5 acres on resistant stock.

*Donzelmann, Wm. M., Calistoga.*—Total, 15 acres; in wine grapes; in bearing, 12 acres; soil mixed; upland; north and south exposure; crop, 23 tons.

*Dorman, John, Santa Rosa.*—Total, 26 acres; all in bearing; soil light loam; upland; exposure, almost level; crop, 52 tons sold and about 30 tons lost by rain.

*Dozier & Pressley, Windsor.*—Total, 39 acres; in wine grapes; in bearing, 25 acres; soil light gravelly loam; valley; southern exposure; crop, 80 tons; cooperage, oak, 10,000 gallons. Fourteen acres of new vineyard planted this spring.

*Dresser, Levi, Santa Rosa.*—Total, 7 acres; all in bearing; low lying; south exposure; crop, 2 tons, rest injured by frost.

*Driscol, T., Santa Rosa.*—Total, 18 acres; in wine grapes; in bearing, 16 acres; soil loam part red, light, and black; upland; east exposure; crop, 40 tons.

*Faught, William, America.*—Total, 15 acres; all in bearing; soil gravelly; upland; exposure south; crop, 12 tons.

*Feige, Rudolph, Fulton.*—Total, 10 acres; all in bearing; soil light gravelly; valley; southern exposure; crop, 20 tons.

*Ford, M., Santa Rosa.*—Total, 30 acres; all in bearing; mostly low lying; crop, 100 tons.

*Fick, Mrs. M., Santa Rosa.*—Total, 20 acres; all in bearing; soil light gravelly; upland; southern exposure; crop, 30 tons.

*Fowler, Miss L. C., Santa Rosa.*—Total, 50 acres; all in bearing; soil gravelly and black loam, also some adobe; upland; exposure, slopes to all points, slightly rolling; crop, 134 tons.
This vineyard shows phylloxera. It has been decided to replant with Lenoir as the old vines die out.

*Fraser, S., Santa Rosa.*—Total, 10 acres; all in bearing; soil loam and adobe; upland; exposure west; crop, 25 tons.

*Fredson, Israel, Windsor.*—Total, 10 acres; all in bearing; soil red loam; upland; southern exposure; crop, 30 tons.
There is a small wine cellar on this place, the cooperage being but a few hundred gallons.

*Frugoli, F., Santa Rosa.*—Total, 25 acres; in wine grapes; in bearing, 15 acres; soil light; low lying; southern exposure; crop, 30 tons.

*Fulton, James, Fulton.*—Total, 5 acres; all in bearing; soil light red loam; low lying; southern exposure; crop, 15 tons.

*Fulterson, Dr. T. S., Santa Rosa.*—Total, 16 acres; all in bearing; soil red loam; upland; southern exposure; crop, 30 tons.

*Fulkerson, S. F., Santa Rosa.*—Total, 23 acres; all in bearing; soil loam, not much gravel; low lying; exposure west and south; crop, 118 tons.

*Fulton Winery Corporation.*—No vineyard, but members of this corporation have wine on hand, 122,000 gallons; cooperage, oak, 17,000 gallons; redwood, 133,000 gallons.

*Garrison, William, Santa Rosa.*—Total, 12 acres; all in bearing; soil light gravelly; mountain; southern exposure; crop, 25 tons.

*Grant, Mrs. Anita Fitch, Healdsburg.*—Total, 30 acres; all in bearing; soil light gravelly; upland; southern exposure; crop, 60 tons.

*Galway, Miss, Santa Rosa.*—Total, 6 acres; all in bearing; soil dark loam; upland; exposure, almost level, full; crop, 20 tons.

*Gem, M. II., Santa Rosa.*—Total, 16 acres; all in bearing; soil light clay; upland; southern exposure; crop, 24 tons.

*Geer, Mrs. Windsor.*—Total, 20 acres; soil light loam; upland; southern exposure; crop, 25 tons.

*Gingery, James, Santa Rosa.*—Total, 12 acres; all in bearing; soil deep loam; upland crop, 18 tons.

*Good, John, Santa Rosa.*—Total, 35 acres; all in bearing; soil gravelly loam and adobe; upland; south and east exposure; crop, 72 tons.

*Goldfish, Wilson & Co., Santa Rosa.*—Total, 32 acres; all in bearing; soil light sandy; low lying; southern exposure; crop, 57 tons.

*Goodman, James T., America.*—Total, 10 acres; all in bearing; soil gravelly loam; mountain; southern exposure; crop, 30 tons.

*Gregg, G. I., Santa Rosa.*—Total, 13 acres; all in bearing; low lying; exposure south and rolling to east and west; crop, 36 tons.

*Greely, Henry, Windsor.*—Total, 113 acres; in wine grapes, 111 acres; in table grapes, 2 acres; soil red loam; sidehills; western exposure; crop, 205 tons. The grapes are shipped to San Francisco, and the wine is made there.

*Grosse, Guy E., Santa Rosa.*—Total, 110 acres; all in bearing; soil deep, red volcanic, basalt, bowlder formation; upland; mountain and summit; north, east, and south exposure; none west except summit; crop, in grapes, 205 tons; wine on hand, 20,000 gallons, comprising vintage of 1887, 1888, 1889, 1890, 1891, and 1892; cooperage, oak, 3,000 gallons; redwood, 7,000 gallons.
Of the above 20,000 gallons wine on hand, 9,000 gallons is in his own cooperage, "Rincon Heights Cellar," and 11,000 gallons is stored in I. DeTurk's cellar, and is in his cooperage, crop of, or vintage of, 1891. He aims to make about 5,000 to 8,000 gallons of wine annually, and sell surplus of grape stock; does not intend to enlarge the capacity of his winery until there is a better price and market assured for California wine. The character of the wine is excellent, the grapes being grown in a favorable locality, free from frosts.

*Grove, D., Windsor.*—Total, 30 acres; all in bearing; soil sandy loam; upland; east slope chiefly, and southeast exposure; crop, 40 tons.

*Guptill, J. II., Santa Rosa.*—Total, 14 acres; in wine grapes, 9 acres; in table grapes, 5 acres; in bearing, 6 acres; soil light loam; upland; exposure south; crop, 11 tons.

*Gunn. J. O'B., Windsor.*—Total, 100 acres; in bearing, 85 acres; soil light sandy; upland; crop, 260 tons; wine on hand, 45,000 gallons; cooperage, oak, 40,000 gallons; redwood, 40,000 gallons. Some vines dying out; looks like phylloxera.

*Gwynn, William, Santa Rosa.*—Total, 40 acres; all in bearing; soil red loam; upland; exposure, all directions; crop, 83 tons.

*Haas, John, Santa Rosa.*—Total, 18 acres; all in bearing; soil loam; upland; exposure south and north; crop, 50 tons; wine on hand, 6,000 gallons; cooperage, oak, 6,000 gallons; redwood, 4,000 gallons.

*Hall, W. A., San Francisco.*—This vineyard is in the Los Guilicos Valley. Total, 42 acres; all in bearing; soil red gravelly; valley; southern exposure; crop, 85 tons.
There are indications of phylloxera in this vineyard, but how badly it is affected is not certain.

*Hanson, August, America.*—Total, 24 acres; in wine grapes; in bearing, 21 acres; soil mixed gravelly loam; upland; exposure east and west; crop, 70 tons.

*Hanson, Peter, Santa Rosa.*—Total, 15 acres; all in bearing; soil red gravelly; upland; exposure southwest and southeast; crop, 90 tons.

*Hardesty, Charles, Santa Rosa.*—Total, 15 acres; all in bearing; soil light gravelly; mountain; southern exposure; crop, 30 tons.

*Harris, Jacob, Santa Rosa.*—Total, 7 acres; all in bearing; soil sandy loam; upland; exposure, all directions; crop, 12 tons.

*Harris, H., Fulton.*—Total, 36 acres; all in bearing; foothills; exposure west and southwest; crop, 95 tons,

*Hasting, F. D., Santa Rosa.*—Total, 25 acres; all in bearing; soil mixed; upland; exposure, all directions; crop, 60 tons.

*Hedrick, D. M., Yulupa.*—Total, 4 acres; all in bearing; soil red gravelly loam; upland; exposure north and west, mountainous on west side; crop, 9 tons.

*Hedrick, L. H., Yulupa.*—Total, 8 acres; all in bearing; soil white gravelly loam; upland; exposure, west slope at the base of Bennett Peak; crop, 16 tons.

*Hefty, Fred., Santa Rosa.*—Total, 15 acres; all in bearing; soil mostly gravelly loam; upland; exposure north and south; crop, 22 tons; cooperage, oak, 20,000 gallons; redwood, 20,000 gallons.

*Heisel, Mrs., Santa Rosa.*—Total, 30 acres; all in bearing; upland; crop, 75 tons.

*Henderson, Mrs. Mary, America.*—Total, 7 acres; all in bearing; soil black; valley; southern exposure; crop, 20 tons.

*Hendly, J. S., Windsor.*—Total, 15 acres; all in bearing; soil light loam; upland; southern exposure; crop, 20 tons.

*Hessel, Andrew, Santa Rosa.*—Total, 40 acres; all in bearing; soil light sandy loam, part gravelly and part clay; upland; almost level, slight southerly slope; crop, 120 tons.

*Hessian, T. H., Santa Rosa.*—Total, 13 acres; all in bearing; soil gray and red loam; upland; east and southeast exposure; crop, 34 tons.

*Higby, L. L., ———.*—Total, 20 acres; all in bearing; soil black loam, some gravel; low lying; southwest exposure; crop, 75 tons.

*Hillman, Mrs. Kate, Santa Rosa.*—Total, 25 acres; all in bearing; soil dark loam; low lying and upland; exposure, slopes gently to the east; crop, 36 tons.

*Holden, J. N., Santa Rosa.*—Total, 8 acres; all in bearing; soil mixed, sandy loam, red and dark; upland; east and west exposure; crop, 31 tons.

*Holland, George, Healdsburg.*—Total, 40 acres; all in bearing; soil light loam; valley; southern exposure; crop, 90 tons.

*Holman, Julius, Santa Rosa.*—Total, 50 acres; all in bearing; soil reddish loam; upland; exposure, all directions; crop, 86 tons.

*Holloway, J. C., Santa Rosa* (Rood place, afterwards Childs).—Total, 35 acres; all in bearing; soil gravelly loam; upland; south and west exposure; crop, 60 tons.

*Hood, Mrs. F. A., South Los Guilicos.*—Total, 230 acres; in wine grapes; in bearing, 105 acres; soil red gravelly; low lying and rolling; south and west exposure; disinfected with bisulphide of carbon, but it proved too expensive; tried flooding with water, but this not practicable; result, will destroy the infected vines and plant resistants; wine on hand, 200,000 gallons; cooperage, oak, 200,000 gallons; redwood, 35,000 gallons. Situated on south base of Hood Mountain, in Los Guilicos Valley, and one of the noted vineyards of the county.

*Hopper, Thomas, Santa Rosa.*—Total, 75 acres; all in bearing; soil loam; upland; western exposure; crop, 200 tons.

*Hotchkiss, W. J., Healdsburg.*—Total, 120 acres; all in bearing; soft red hill; upland; exposure, all directions; no resistant stock, and no evidence of phylloxera; crop, 200 tons; wine on hand, 7,000 gallons; cooperage, oak, 1,500 gallons; redwood, 75,000 gallons.

*Howe, E. A., Fulton.*—Total, 8 acres; all in bearing; soil light clay; valley; southern exposure; crop, 15 tons.

*Hudson (heirs of), Santa Rosa.*—Total, 20 acres; all in bearing; soil light loam; valley; southern exposure; crop, 18 tons.

*Hulett, H. C., Santa Rosa,*—Total, 18 acres; all in bearing; soil gravelly loam; upland; northern exposure; crop, 50 tons.

*Hunger, Felix, Santa Rosa.*—Total, 16 acres; all in bearing; soil red volcanic; mountain; western exposure; crop, 30 tons.

*Hunter, J. E., Santa Rosa.*—Total, 10 acres; all in bearing; soil mixed sandy, gravelly loam; upland; exposure very little; crop, 36 tons.

*Irvine, A., San Francisco.*—Vineyard near Fulton. Total, 12 acres; all in bearing; soil light clay; valley; southern exposure; crop, 15 tons.

*Jacobson, J. H., Windsor.*—Total, 17 acres; in wine grapes; in bearing, 12 acres; soil red gravelly; upland; crop, 44 tons. So far the vines are healthy around Windsor, and no resistants have been planted.

*Juilliard, L. W., Santa Rosa.*—Total, 30 acres; all in bearing; soil red gravelly; mountain; eastern exposure; crop, 50 tons.

*Kauffman, J., Santa Rosa.*—Total, 10 acres; all in bearing; soil mixed loam; upland; level and easterly exposure; crop, 15 tons.

*Kelley, J. W., Sebastopol.*—Total, 25 acres; all in bearing; soil red; valley; southern exposure; crop, 40 tons.

*Keeler, John, Windsor.*—Total, 22 acres; all in bearing; soil red gravelly; upland; exposure, all directions; crop, 50 tons.

*Kenwood Land Company, Los Guilicos.*—Total, 50 acres; in table grapes; all in bearing; soil light; valley and hill; northern and southern exposure; a young vineyard, planted this season in the hills south of Santa Rosa Creek.

*Kise, Mrs., Windsor.*—Total, 5 acres; all in bearing; soil gravelly loam; low lying; southerly exposure; crop, 18 tons.

*Kirch, Mrs. H., Santa Rosa.*—Total, 60 acres; in wine grapes, 40 acres; in bearing, 40 acres; soil black; upland; exposure, all directions; crop, 100 tons.

*Klotz, Mrs. C. G., Calistoga.*—Total, 25 acres; all in bearing; soil volcanic and mixed; upland; exposure, all directions; crop, 55 tons; wine all sold but 1,000 gallons; cooperage, oak, 5,000 gallons; redwood, 15,000 gallons.

*Knapp, Mrs. M. A., Santa Rosa.*—Total, 85 acres; all in bearing; soil light loam; upland; exposure south; crop, 190 tons.

*Kunde, Charles L., Windsor.*—Total, 11 acres; in wine grapes; in bearing, 10 acres; soil gravelly loam; upland; westerly exposure; crop, 34 tons saved, lost much by rotting. This is a very pretty, well-cared-for vineyard. Vines all healthy and looking vigorous. Has planted one acre of resistants as an experiment.

*Laughlin, Lee, Windsor.*—Total, 10 acres; all in bearing; soil gravelly; mountain; western exposure; crop, 25 tons.

*Laveroni, John, Windsor.*—Total, 12 acres; in wine grapes; in bearing, 8 acres; soil light loam; upland; southern exposure; crop, 25 tons.

*Largomasini, B., Santa Rosa.*—Total, 20 acres; all in bearing; soil clay loam; upland; exposure south; crop, 22 tons; wine on hand, 5,000 gallons; cooperage, redwood, 6,000 gallons.

*Laughlin, John (estate of), America.*—Total, 10 acres; all in bearing; soil light loam; valley; southern exposure; crop, 20 tons.

*Laughlin, Mrs. J. H., Mark West.*—Total, 30 acres; in wine grapes, 25 acres; in table grapes, 5 acres; upland; crop, 75 tons.

*Latimer, L. D., Windsor.*—Total, 46 acres; all in bearing; soil mostly deep, grayish loam, with reddish friable clay underlying; upland; exposure south and west; crop, 160 tons.

*Lay, Clark & Co., "Fountain Grove," Santa Rosa.*—Total, 400 acres; in wine grapes, 375 acres; in table grapes, 25 acres; soil red, ashy, sandy loam and hill adobe; upland; exposure, all directions; crop, 1,500 tons; wine on hand, 250,000 gallons; cooperage, oak, 300,000 gallons.

*Lacque, B. F., Santa Rosa.*—Total, 20 acres; all in bearing, soil white loam; upland; southeast exposure; crop, 70 tons.

*Lawler, John, Santa Rosa.*—Total, 12 acres; all in bearing; soil black loam; upland; exposure north; crop, 30 tons.

*Lehn, Chas., Windsor.*—Total, 26 acres; all in bearing; soil gravelly; upland; southern exposure; crop, 60 tons.

*Leverone, J., Windsor.*—Total, 15 acres; in wine grapes; in bearing, 2 acres; soil clay loam; upland; exposure, full; crop, 3 tons.
This is a young vineyard, 13 acres having been planted this year.

*Lock, J. N., Santa Rosa.*—Total, 10 acres; all in bearing; soil gravelly loam; upland; south, east, and west exposure; crop, 30 tons.

*Luce, W. Y., Healdsburg.*—Total, 22 acres; all in bearing; soil black loam and light gravelly; mountain and valley; south and east exposure; crop, 100 tons.
This is a good vineyard, at eastern base of Fitch Mountain, surrounded on three sides by Russian River.

*Macartney, A. H. E., South Los Guilicos.*—Total, 80 acres; all in bearing; soil gravelly loam; hill and low lying; southern and western exposure; crop, 170 tons. This vineyard is situated in Los Guilicos Valley, at southern base of Hood Mountain. Phylloxera in spots only; a good vineyard, and but little affected.

*Madsen, Mrs. M. M., Fulton.*—Total, 8 acres; all in bearing; soil light clay; low lying; southern exposure; crop, 22 tons.

*Man, Christian, Santa Rosa.*—Total, 6 acres; all in bearing; soil light; southern exposure; crop, 30 tons.

*Manion, Mrs., Santa Rosa.*—Total, 20 acres; all in bearing; soil part gravelly loam, part red, part adobe; part upland and part low lying; north and west exposure; crop, 48 tons.

*Mardis, L. W., Santa Rosa.*—Total, 43 acres; in wine grapes, 38 acres; in table grapes, 5 acres; soil red gravelly loam; low lying; exposure, very little inclination; crop, 76 tons wine grapes.

*Martin, M. E., Windsor.*—Total, 5 acres; all in bearing; soil light loam; upland; southern exposure; crop, 10 tons.

*McCann, Mrs. E., Santa Rosa.*—Total, 30 acres; all in bearing; soil light loam; mountain; southern exposure; crop, 80 tons.

*McCutchen, W. C., Windsor.*—Total, 10 acres; all in bearing; soil gravelly red; upland; exposure, all directions; crop, 12 tons.

*McCutchen, William, Windsor.*—Total, 15 acres; all in bearing; soil light loam; upland; southern exposure; crop, 40 tons.

*McCoy, C. L., "Riverside Farm," Healdsburg.*—Total, 25 acres; in wine grapes, 23 acres; in table grapes, 2 acres; soil reddish loam; upland; southwest exposure; crop, 83 tons; wine on hand, 8,000 gallons; cooperage, redwood, 60,000 gallons.

*McGregor, F. D., Santa Rosa.*—Total, 30 acres; all in bearing; soil light red gravel; rolling hill; southern exposure; crop, 43 tons.

*McIsaacs, Alex., Santa Rosa.*—Total, 8 acres; all in bearing; soil loam; upland; exposure, all directions; crop, 32 tons. Phylloxera noticed in this vineyard last year for the first time.

*McKeadney, H., Healdsburg.*—Total, 38 acres; all in bearing; soil red loam; hill; southern exposure; crop, 127 tons.

*Mathison, H. P., Santa Rosa.*—Total, 8 acres; all in bearing; soil light loam; upland; exposure, almost level; crop, 20 tons.
Many of the vines in this vineyard dying; have been dying for two years, but not certain that their death is caused by phylloxera; does not so appear.

*Meacham, A., Fulton.*—Total, 15 acres; all in bearing; soil light ashy soil; rolling valley; southern exposure; crop, 37 tons.

*Medeiros, J. R., Santa Rosa.*—Total, 5 acres; all in bearing; soil light; low lying; southern exposure; crop, 25 tons.

*Mee, Mrs. A. C., Calistoga.*—Total, 12 acres; all in bearing; soil gravelly and black loam; upland; exposure, all directions; crop, 10 tons.

*Michaelson, George, Windsor.*—Total, 14 acres; all in bearing; soil light gravelly loam; upland; western exposure; crop, 30 tons.

*Miller, James R., Windsor.*—Total, 35 acres; all in bearing; soil light loam; part valley and part upland; south and west exposure; crop, 65 tons.

*Milton (heirs of), Windsor.*—Total, 38 acres; all in bearing; soil light gravelly; valley; southern exposure; crop, 120 tons.

*Miller, G. F., Fulton.*—Total, 18 acres; all in bearing; soil light loam; low lying; southern exposure; crop, 40 tons.

*Miller, G. R., Santa Rosa.*—Total, 15 acres; all in bearing; soil loam; upland; exposure, nearly level; crop, 25 tons; wine on hand, 3,500 gallons; cooperage, oak, 1,000 gallons; redwood, 4,500 gallons.

*Miller, Jeannette, Santa Rosa.*—Total, 7 acres; all in bearing; soil light loam; low bottom; crop, 10 tons.

*Minna, John, Santa Rosa.*—Total, 10 acres; all in bearing; soil loam; upland; southern exposure; crop, 8 tons; many spoiled on vines.

*Moore, H., Santa Rosa.*—Total, 10 acres; in wine grapes, 9 acres; in table grapes, 1 acre; soil gravelly loam; upland; exposure west; crop, 25 tons.

*Morgan, George, Windsor.*—Total, 10 acres; all in bearing; soil gravelly; upland; western exposure; crop, 20 tons.

*Morrow, James, Santa Rosa.*—Total, 10 acres; all in bearing; soil black loam and adobe; upland; northerly exposure; crop, 18 tons.

*Murdock, L. A., Santa Rosa.*—Total, 70 acres; all in bearing; soil loam; upland; exposure south and east; crop, 180 tons.

*Meyers, D. P., Windsor.*—Total, 18 acres; in wine grapes, 17 acres; in table grapes, 1 acre; soil, one half volcanic and one half alluvial; mountain; southern exposure; crop, 45 tons; wine on hand, 5,000 gallons; cooperage, oak, 3,500 gallons; redwood, 7,000 gallons.

*Marsh, Mrs., Santa Rosa.*—Total, 22 acres; all in bearing; soil black loam; upland; exposure, nearly level; crop, 80 tons; wine on hand, 10,000 gallons; cooperage, redwood, 12,000 gallons.
M. A. Pacheco owns the winery on this place.

*Nagle, G. F., Santa Rosa.*—Total, 30 acres; in wine grapes, 29 acres; in table grapes, 1 acre; soil light clay; low lying; exposure east, south, and west; crop, 63 tons; about 30 tons rotted.

*Near, Chas., Santa Rosa.*—Total, 25 acres; all in bearing; soil black loam; upland; exposure, hills sloping in nearly all directions; crop, 100 tons; some rotted on the vines.

*Norris, Mrs. M. E., Santa Rosa.*—Total, 28 acres; all in bearing; soil, part gravelly and part clay loam; upland; exposure south and west; crop, 90 tons.

*Ode, Peter, Healdsburg.*—Total, 20 acres; all in bearing; soil light loam; upland; southern exposure; crop, 60 tons. ·

*O'Neil, Eugene, Oakland* (vineyard near Healdsburg).—Total, 20 acres; all in bearing; soil gravelly loam; upland; southern exposure; crop, 16 tons.

*Ortman, Thomas, "Ross Place," Healdsburg.*—Total, 13 acres; all in bearing; soil light gravelly; valley; southern exposure; crop, 14 tons.

*Packwood, A. J., Windsor.*—Total, 10 acres; all in bearing; soil gravelly loam; low lying; crop, 35 tons.
Mr. Packwood expects to change from grapes to prunes, as land is more suitable for fruit, and grape prices not being satisfactory.

*Palos Grande Coal Manufacturing Co., Santa Rosa.*—Total, 34 acres; all in bearing; soil gravelly loam and adobe; upland; exposure east and south; crop, 50 tons.

*Pepper, O. T., Santa Rosa.*—Total, 20 acres; all in bearing; soil light gravelly; upland; western exposure; crop, 57 tons.

*Peter, Jesse, Santa Rosa.*—Total, 20 acres; all in bearing; soil red adobe; low lying; exposure, level; crop, 8 tons, not much picked.

*Peterson, Captain A., Santa Rosa.*—Total, 22 acres; all in bearing; soil light loam; rolling; southern exposure; crop, 40 tons.

*Peterson, Edwin, Yulupa.*—Total, 8 acres; all in bearing; soil black loam; upland; exposure, west slope, Bennett Peak on east; crop, 30 tons.

*Petry, R. A., Healdsburg.*—Total, 21 acres; all in bearing; soil black and red loam; level; crop, 60 tons. Neither suckered, sulphured, nor hoed. From 6 to 10 tons mildewed or blighted.

*Pfhingston, John, and Hemker, Henry, Santa Rosa.*—Total, 14 acres; all in bearing; soil, light sandy loam and part red gravelly loam; upland; exposure, slopes slightly to the south; crop, 40 tons.

*Phillips, Walter, Santa Rosa.*—Total, 140 acres; all in bearing; soil clay adobe; upland; exposure in every direction; crop, 300 tons; wine on hand, 80,000 gallons; cooperage, oak, 50,000 gallons; redwood, 30,000 gallons. Best grapes and best wine on north slope.
This vineyard is properly cultivated and cared for, and is one of the best in Bennett Valley.

*Philpott, B. F., Windsor.*—Total, 5 acres; all in bearing; soil black loam; valley; southern exposure; crop, 10 tons.

*Piezzi, Victor, Santa Rosa.*—Total, 25 acres; all in bearing; soil red loam, part sandy; upland; exposure, slightly rolling north and south; crop, 90 tons; made 8,000 gallons wine and sold 15 tons grapes; wine on hand, 3,800 gallons; cooperage, oak, 1,500 gallons; redwood, 5,000 gallons.

*Pitts, John, America.*—Total, 7 acres; all in bearing; soil gravelly loam; mountain; exposure north.

*Polifka, Charles, Santa Rosa.*—Total, 10 acres; all in bearing; soil sandy loam; valley; southern exposure; crop, 32 tons; wine on hand, 5,000 gallons; cooperage, oak, 2,000 gallons; redwood, 3,000 gallons.

*Porter, James, Santa Rosa.*—Total, 9 acres; all in bearing; soil loam; upland; exposure, almost level; crop, 16 tons.

*Poulin, L., Santa Rosa.*—Total, 7 acres; all in bearing; soil mixed, some black, some gravelly, and some adobe; upland; exposure, north and west slopes principally; crop, 35 tons; wine on hand, 6,500 gallons; cooperage, oak, 3,500 gallons; redwood, 8,000 gallons.

*Pressley, J. G., Santa Rosa.*—Total, 25 acres; all in bearing; soil gravelly; mountain; south and west exposure; crop, 50 tons.

*Ralston, A. J., Santa Rosa.*—Total, 25 acres; all in bearing; soil loam; upland; south exposure; crop, 7 tons were gathered.

*Requa, Arthur A., Santa Rosa.*—Total, 29 acres; all in bearing; soil red volcanic; mountain; exposure, north slope; crop, 23 tons; wine on hand, sold, but not delivered, 11,000 gallons; cooperage, oak, 3,000 gallons; redwood, 12,000 gallons. At this winery are solid stone fermenting tanks, holding about 8,000 gallons.

*Rend, J. C., San Francisco.*—This winery is near Windsor. Total, 8 acres; in wine grapes; in bearing, 5 acres; soil light loam; upland; southern exposure; crop, 10 tons.

*Riley, A., Santa Rosa.*—Total, 20 acres; all in bearing; soil red loam; mountain; exposure, level and east slope; crop, 40 tons.
There is phylloxera in this vineyard; will replant with Lenoir.

*Roberts, Frank, Santa Rosa.*—Total, 15 acres; all in bearing; soil red loam; mountain; south exposure; crop, 40 tons.

*Ross, Richard, Santa Rosa.*—Total, 26 acres; all in bearing; soil gravelly loam; upland; south exposure; crop, 60 tons.

*Runyan, H. L., Windsor.*—Total, 11 acres; all in bearing; soil gravelly and adobe; upland; south exposure; crop, 18 tons.

*Sachs, Martin, San Francisco.*—The vineyard is at the east side of the county, part of it being in Napa County. Total, 100 acres; all in bearing; soil light gravelly; mountain; southern exposure; crop, 200 tons; wine on hand, 50,000 gallons.

*Santa Rosa Bank, Santa Rosa.*—Total, 75 acres; all in bearing; soil sandy loam; upland; exposure south; crop, 250 tons.

*Schwan, L., Santa Rosa.*—Total, 20 acres; all in bearing; soil red; mountain; northern exposure; crop, 30 tons.

*Scheibel, Th., Yulupa.*—Total, 30 acres; all in bearing; soil gravelly loam and adobe; upland; exposure, east slope, mountain on west side; crop, 45 tons; wine on hand, 3,000 gallons; cooperage, oak, 1,500 gallons; redwood, 4,500 gallons.

*Schelish, Antone, Santa Rosa.*—Total, 10 acres; in wine grapes; in bearing, 8 acres; soil black loam; upland; exposure, all directions; crop, 22 tons.

*Seward, Joshua, Fulton.*—Total, 15 acres; all in bearing; soil dark loam; valley; southern exposure; crop, 75 tons.

*Sheplar, S. H., Santa Rosa.*—Total, 30 acres; soil black loam; low lying; crop, 60 tons.

*Sharp, Charles C., America.*—Total, 7 acres; all in bearing; soil clay loam; mountain; crop, 25 tons.

*Sharp, Nathan, America.*—Total, 8 acres; all in bearing; soil clay loam; upland and mountain; exposure south and north; crop, 35 tons.

*Shooks, A. L., Santa Rosa.*—Total, 5 acres; all in bearing; soil gravelly; upland; exposure north; crop, 4 tons.

*Siemer, D., Santa Rosa.*—Total, 17 acres; in wine grapes; in bearing, 10 acres; soil mixed loam; upland; exposure, slightly rolling; crop, 40 tons; wine on hand, 5,000 gallons; cooperage, oak, 1,500 gallons; redwood, 4,000 gallons.

*Smith, F., Healdsburg.*—Total, 30 acres; in wine grapes; in bearing, 25 acres; soil red gravelly; valley; southern exposure; crop, 120 tons; cooperage, redwood, 40,000 gallons.

*Slusser, Thomas, Mark West.*—Total, 10 acres; all in bearing; soil slight loam; valley; southern exposure; crop, 15 tons.

*Smithers, G. E., Santa Rosa.*—Total, 6 acres; in wine grapes, 4 acres; in table grapes, 2 acres; soil sandy loam; upland; exposure, slopes north; crop, 11 tons.

*Stewart, J. II., Santa Rosa.*—Total, 10 acres; in wine grapes, 7½ acres; in table grapes, 2½ acres; soil gravelly loam; upland; exposure north; slopes slightly; crop, 11 tons.

*Stridde, A. W., Santa Rosa.*—Total, 12 acres; all in bearing; soil gravelly loam; upland; exposure, west slope; crop, 18 tons.

*Strong, John, Santa Rosa.*—Total, 50 acres; all in bearing; soil gravelly loam; upland; exposure, all directions; crop, 108 tons.

*Story, S. C., Santa Rosa.*—Total, 20 acres; all in bearing; soil mixed, part adobe; upland; exposure, all directions; crop, 86 tons; wine on hand, 12,300 gallons; cooperage, redwood, 13,000 gallons.

*Stuart (estate of), Santa Rosa.*—Total, 60 acres; all in bearing; soil mixed, gravelly, etc.; upland; exposure, mostly west slope; crop, 160 tons.

*Stridde, Chas., Santa Rosa.*—Total, 40 acres; all in bearing; soil red and black; upland; exposure south and west; crop, 128 tons.

*Stewarts, A., Fulton.*—Total, 6 acres; all in bearing; soil light gravelly; valley; southern exposure; crop, 12 tons.

*Sutherland, R. II., Santa Rosa.*—Total, 30 acres; all in bearing; soil sandy loam; upland and rolling; exposure generally south; crop, 115 tons sold, some decayed on vines. Phylloxera has injured the vineyard somewhat the past three years. Has taken out about 2 acres of affected vines, but has not replanted.

*Tarwater, II. A., America.*—Total, 27 acres; in wine grapes, 25 acres; in table grapes, 2 acres; soil heavy red; upland and mountain; westerly exposure; crop, 50 tons.

*Taylor, J. S., Santa Rosa.*—Total, 60 acres; all in bearing; soil gravelly loam; upland; western exposure; crop, 135 tons.

*Tauzer, Albert, Santa Rosa.*—Total, 17 acres; all in bearing; soil light loam; upland and low lying; exposure, all directions; crop, 21 tons; wine on hand, 5,000 gallons; cooperage, oak, 2,500 gallons; redwood, 4,500 gallons.

*Talbott, II., Santa Rosa.*—Total, 12 acres; all in bearing; soil volcanic loam; upland; exposure south; crop, 50 tons.

*Talbott, Jas., Santa Rosa.*—Total, 20 acres; all in bearing; soil volcanic loam; upland; exposure south; crop, 100 tons.

*Thorpe, R. W., Santa Rosa.*—Total, 13 acres; all in bearing; soil light clay; upland; southern and western exposure; crop, 16 tons. Mr. Thorpe talks of pulling out his vines and of planting the ground to something else, unless the vineyard business improves soon.

*Traver, J. C., Santa Rosa.*—Total, 15 acres; all in bearing; soil light loam; valley; southern exposure; crop, 35 tons

*Underhill, J. G., Charles, and W. II., Santa Rosa.*—Total, 40 acres; all in bearing; soil black loam; upland; exposure south; crop, 96 tons.

*Van Keppel, Henry, Santa Rosa.*—Total, 27 acres; all in bearing; soil black loam and adobe; upland; exposure east; crop, 80 tons.

*Van Winkle, Mrs. W. P., Fulton.*—Total, 18 acres; all in bearing; soil light gravelly; upland; western exposure; crop, 29 tons.

*Valdes, Mercedes, Santa Rosa.*—Total, 13 acres; all in bearing; soil loam; upland; exposure, slight slope to east; crop, 38 tons.

*Van Grafan, Chas., Santa Rosa.*—Total, 10 acres; all in bearing; soil black loam, red, sandy and little adobe; upland exposure west slope; crop, 25 tons. Mr. Van Grafan says that where vines get root in adobe they do best; they are more difficult to start in adobe soil, but he gets best results there when they were well started.

*Velargo, John, Santa Rosa.*—Total, 10 acres; all in bearing; soil red sandy loam; upland; exposure, slopes north; crop, 19 tons.

*Watson, J. T., Windsor.*—Total, 8 acres; all in bearing; soil light loam; upland; southern exposure; crop, 25 tons.

*Walker, D. W., Fulton.*—Total, 8 acres; all in bearing; soil light clay; valley; exposure south; crop, 40 tons.

*Ward, N., Healdsburg.*—Total, 60 acres; all in bearing; soil light loam; upland; exposure west and south; crop, 150 tons.

*Ware, A. B., Santa Rosa.*—Total, 65 acres; all in bearing; soil light clay; rolling; southern exposure; crop, 205 tons.

*Wells, C., Santa Rosa.*—Total, 16 acres; all in bearing; soil gravelly loam; upland; exposure west; crop, 38 tons.

*Wells, Pleasant, Santa Rosa.*—Total, 150 acres; in bearing, 140 acres; in wine grapes, 146 acres; in table grapes, 4 acres; soil dark red; upland; exposure north and south; crop, 325 tons.
Mr. Wells has sold his grapes heretofore, but he is now building a winery and expects to make wine in the future.

*Wells, George, Santa Rosa.*—Total, 8 acres; all in bearing; soil loam; upland; exposure west; crop, 17 tons.

*Wheeler Bros., Santa Rosa.*—Total, 35 acres; all in bearing; soil red loam; upland; exposure, all directions; crop, 63 tons.

*Weeks, S. S., Santa Rosa.*—Total, 6 acres; all in bearing; soil light clay; low lying; southern and eastern exposure; crop, 6 tons.

*Wendt, Fred., Santa Rosa.*—Total, 7 acres; all in bearing; soil light gravelly; mountain; southern exposure; crop, 15 tons.

*Whitaker, G. N., Santa Rosa.*—Total, 50 acres; all in bearing; soil light sandy loam; upland; exposure east and north; crop, 150 tons; wine on hand, 30,000 gallons; cooperage, oak, 23,000 gallons; redwood, 12,000 gallons.
This vineyard is well up on the south slope of Taylor Mountain. It is well cared for, and the vines are healthy, vigorous, and productive.

*Wilson, M. A., Windsor.*—Total, 20 acres; all in bearing; soil light gravelly; mountain; southern exposure; crop, 60 tons.

*Wilson, Mr., Santa Rosa.*—Total, 20 acres; all in bearing; soil red; mountain; exposure, nearly level; crop, 20 tons. The amount produced, an estimate. The grapes were not weighed, but were dried on the place.

*Wood, Wesley, Fulton.*—Total, 7 acres; all in bearing; soil red gravelly loam; upland; exposure, slightly to the southeast; crop, 14 tons.

*Wolf, A., San Francisco* (vineyard near Mark West Creek, five miles north of Santa Rosa).—Total, 9 acres; all in bearing; soil loam; upland; southern and western exposure; crop, 20 tons.

*Wright, Adam, Fulton.*—Total, 20 acres; all in bearing; soil light gravelly; valley; southern exposure; crop, 25 tons.

*Wright, W. M. (estate of), Calistoga.*—Total, 5 acres; all in bearing; soil white volcanic; mountain; exposure, slopes a little to the east; crop, 20 tons.

*Yetes, J. W., Windsor.*—Total, 12 acres; all in bearing; soil light loam; valley; southern exposure; crop, 37 tons.

# FOURTH DISTRICT.

COMPRISING THE TOWNSHIPS OF CLOVERDALE, KNIGHTS VALLEY, MENDOCINO, AND WASHINGTON.

*Albee, Mrs. H. T., Cloverdale.*—Total, 11 acres; all in bearing; soil light; upland; southern exposure; crop, 40 tons.

*Alexander, Thomas, Littons.*—Total, 30 acres; all in bearing; soil light sandy loam; valley; exposure east and south; crop, 100 tons.

*Algreen, George, Healdsburg.*—Total, 5 acres; all in bearing; soil light gravelly; upland; eastern exposure; crop, 10 tons.

*Andreazzi & Monico, Geyserville.*—Total, 30 acres, all in bearing; soil light gravelly; mountain; eastern exposure; crop, 100 tons.

*Ardieu, P., Healdsburg.*—Total, 10 acres; all in bearing; soil light gravelly; mountain; northern exposure; crop, 35 tons.

*Archembeau Estate, Geyserville.*—Total, 20 acres; all in bearing; soil light loam; valley; eastern and southern exposure; crop, 84 tons.

The vineyard is situated in the valley at base of hills on west side of Russian River, above Geyserville; some vines dying, whether from phylloxera or not could not be ascertained; there is phylloxera in this neighborhood.

*Armstrong, J. B., Cloverdale.*—Total, 6 acres; all in bearing; soil light gravelly; upland; eastern exposure; crop, 30 tons.

*Arthur, D., Alexander Valley.*—Total, 15 acres; all in bearing; soil light gravelly; upland; southern exposure; crop, 25 tons.

*Axford, William, Healdsburg.*—Total, 10 acres; all in bearing; soil gravelly; upland; southern exposure; crop, 25 tons.

*Bank of Healdsburg, Healdsburg.*—Total, 275 acres; in wine grapes, 225 acres; in table grapes, 50 acres; soil varied; valley and hill; exposure, protected by foothills; crop, 700 tons. This vineyard is situated in Alexander Valley, and was formerly the Mulligan place.

*Bailey, W. H., Healdsburg.*—Total, 18 acres; all in bearing; soil red; upland; southern exposure; crop, 40 tons.

*Baker, A. M., Healdsburg.*—Total, 12 acres; all in bearing; soil light gravelly; upland; exposure north and east; crop, 40 tons.

*Bailey, W. H., Alexander Valley.*—Total, 35 acres; all in bearing; soil red; upland; northern exposure; crop, 126 tons.

*Beeson, W. S., Healdsburg.*—Total, 8 acres; all in bearing; soil gravelly loam; upland; exposure, slopes south; crop, 25 tons.

*Bennett, Mrs. E., Geyserville.*—Total, 20 acres; all in bearing; soil black loam; upland; western exposure; crop, 100 tons.

*Bell, J. S., Healdsburg.*—Total, 20 acres; all in bearing; soil black loam; valley; northern exposure; crop, 70 tons.

*Bell, A. K., Healdsburg.*—Total, 15 acres; all in bearing; soil black loam; valley; northern exposure; crop, 60 tons.

*Bell, J. W., Healdsburg.*—Total, 20 acres; all in bearing; soil red gravelly; upland; southern exposure; crop, 60 tons.
Mr. Bell's place is located on the south side of Dry Creek, near Pina Creek, and is a good vineyard.

*Bidwell, James, Soda Rock.*—Total, 15 acres; all in bearing; soil light gravelly; upland; southern exposure; crop, 40 tons.

*Bidwell, John, Soda Rock.*—Total, 15 acres; all in bearing; crop, 40 tons.

*Bice, Mrs., Healdsburg.*—Total, 8 acres; all in bearing; soil red gravelly; upland; eastern exposure; crop, 25 tons.

*Black, W. A., Healdsburg.*—Total, 9 acres; all in bearing; soil red gravelly; lowland; easterly exposure; crop, 31 tons.

*Black, W. H., Cloverdale.*—Total, 45 acres; in wine grapes; in bearing, 20 acres; red soil and valley; upland and valley; exposure west and south; crop, 100 tons.
Mr. Black has 25 acres of new vineyard and 20 acres of old vines in river bottom. The vines are all healthy and vigorous and promise a big crop. His place is situated across Russian River, opposite the Swiss-Italian Colony.

*Bledsoe, A. C., Healdsburg.*—Total, 18 acres; all in bearing; soil, clay in the main; upland; exposure, all directions; crop, 70 tons.
Mr. Bledsoe's place is situated in the hills on the north side of Russian River.

*Bonner, Robert, Cozzens.*—Total, 15 acres; all in bearing; soil light loam; valley; southern exposure; crop, 75 tons; has a small wine cellar.

*Bourdens, P., Skaggs Spring.*—Total, 8 acres; all in bearing; soil part red gravelly loam and part clay; hill sloping to north on mountain; southern exposure; crop, 11 tons; wine on hand, 200 gallons; cooperage, oak, 700 gallons; redwood, 300 gallons.

*Bonman, Mrs. I. W., Cloverdale.*—Total, 6 acres; all in bearing; soil clay; lowland; westerly exposure; crop, 6 tons.

*Bosworth, C. M., Geyserville.*—Total, 40 acres; in wine grapes, 38 acres; in raisin grapes, 2 acres; soil gravelly and clay loam; upland; southern exposure; crop, 100 tons.

*Board, William, Healdsburg.*—Total, 10 acres; all in bearing; soil black; valley; northern exposure; crop, 40 tons.

*Board, H. D., Cozzens.*—Total, 8 acres; all in bearing; soil red; upland; southern exposure; crop, nothing, this being a young vineyard just set out on red hills on south side of Dry Creek above Cozzens.

*Boyds, Thos., Cozzens.*—Total, 7 acres; all in bearing; soil light loam; valley; southern exposure; crop, 30 tons.

*Bradford, R. A., Healdsburg.*—Total, 21 acres; all in bearing; soil gravel and clay; valley; exposure south and east; crop, 44 tons.

*Brigham, G. H., Healdsburg.*—Total, 9 acres; all in bearing; soil red; valley; southern exposure; crop, 25 tons.

*Bradford, D. J., Healdsburg.*—Total, 18 tons; all in bearing; soil gravel and clay; valley; exposure north and east; crop, 30 tons.

*Brown, Samuel, Healdsburg.*—Total, 14 acres; all in bearing; soil light loam; upland; southern exposure; crop, 48 tons.
The vineyard is in the hills to the north of Healdsburg.

*Bryant Bros., Cozzens.*—Total, 10 acres; all in bearing; soil light loam; upland; southern exposure; crop, 40 tons.

*Bryant, D. S., Healdsburg.*—Total, 12 acres; all in bearing; soil red loam; upland; southern exposure; crop, 40 tons.

*Burnham, A. E., Healdsburg.*—Total, 16 acres; in wine grapes; in bearing, 15 acres; soil black gravel; upland; crop, 60 tons.
This vineyard is in Dry Creek Valley, and is well cultivated and very thrifty.

*Burke, Mrs. M., Healdsburg.*—Total, 19 acres; all in bearing; soil deep sandy loam; upland; crop, 67 tons.

*Burr, Frank, Geyserville.*—Total, 30 acres; in wine grapes, 26 acres; in table grapes, 2 acres; in raisin grapes, 2 acres; soil sandy loam; exposure east; crop, 100 tons.

*Butterfield, James, Healdsburg.*—Total, 5 acres; all in bearing; soil light loam; upland; exposure north and east; crop, 10 tons.

*Byrod, Mrs., Oakland.*—Total, 18 acres; all in bearing; soil red; upland; southern exposure; crop, 40 tons.

*Caldwell, William, Cloverdale.*—Total, 55 acres; all in bearing; soil light loam; lowland; southern exposure; crop, 150 tons.

*Callahan, J., Healdsburg.*—Total, 10 acres; in wine grapes, 7½ acres; in table grapes, 1 acre; in raisin grapes, 1½ acres; soil inclined to adobe; upland; exposure south and north; crop, 35 tons.
This place is in the hills north of Russian River.

*Carter, M. M., Calistoga.*—Total, 18 acres; in wine grapes, 17 acres; in table grapes, 1 acre; soil red; mountain; exposure south and west; crop, 46 tons.

*Champion, John, Cloverdale.*—Total, 60 acres; all in bearing; soil red gravelly; upland; westerly exposure; crop, 120 tons.

*Clausen & Terkildsen, Cozzens.*—Total, 20 acres; in wine grapes, 17 acres; in table grapes, 3 acres; soil gravelly loam; low lying; crop, 90 tons.

*Clark, Mrs. R. M., Healdsburg.*—Total, 4 acres; all in bearing; soil red loam; upland; southern exposure; crop, 15 tons.

*Coghill, ——, Healdsburg.*—Total, 30 acres; all in bearing; soil red; upland; northern exposure; crop, 75 tons.

*Codding, Geo. P., Healdsburg.*—Total, 10 acres; all in bearing; soil light gravelly; mountain; southern exposure; crop, 25 tons.

*Coulson, Nicholas, Healdsburg.*—Total, 12 acres; all in bearing; soil red loam; hill; northern exposure; crop, 40 tons.

*Coulson, John, Healdsburg.*—Total, 35 acres; all in bearing; soil red; upland; northern exposure; crop, 100 tons.

*Coomes, A. M., Cloverdale.*—Total, 13 acres; in wine grapes, 3 acres; in table grapes, 10 acres; soil black loam; valley; southern exposure; crop, 40 tons.

*Cooley, C. H. & J. B., Cloverdale.*—Total, 60 acres; in wine grapes, 56 acres; in table grapes, 4 acres; soil red, sandy, and clay; low lying; westerly exposure; crop, 100 tons.

*Cozzens, D., Cozzens.*—Total, 8 acres; all in bearing; soil gravelly; foothills; crop, 25 tons.

*Crocker, ——, Geyserville.*—Total, 22 acres; in wine grapes, 17 acres; in table grapes, 4 acres; in raisin grapes, 1 acre; soil for wine grapes is gravelly loam, for table grapes, clayey; upland; easterly exposure; crop, 83 tons.

*Crocker, H. J., Cloverdale.*—Total, 50 acres; all in bearing; soil red and dark loam; mountain; southern exposure; crop, 100 tons.

*Cunningham, J., Cloverdale.*—Total, 10 acres; all in bearing; soil gravelly; mountain; southern exposure; crop, 20 tons.

*Cummings, J. M., Geyserville.*—Total, 12 acres; all in bearing; soil light gravel; low lying; eastern exposure; crop, 45 tons.

*Dehay, Armand, Cloverdale.*—Total, 38 acres; all in bearing; soil light gravelly loam; valley; exposure north and east; crop, 120 tons. Of this vineyard, 8 acres come into bearing this year.

*Dehay, T. J., Cloverdale.*—Total, 23 acres; all in bearing; soil light loam; upland; eastern exposure; crop, 70 tons; has a small winery and distillery; cooperage, oak, 5,000 gallons; redwood, 30,000 gallons.

*Delafield, R. H., Calistoga.*—Total, 35 acres; all in bearing; soil red loam; mountain; northern exposure; crop, 80 tons.
This vineyard is located on a range of mountains on the south side of Knights Valley, near the petrified forest. There is a good stone wine cellar at this vineyard.

*Denari, A., Geyserville.*—Total, 45 acres; in wine grapes; in bearing, 30 acres; soil red; upland; eastern exposure; crop, 50 tons; all his wine has been sold; cooperage, redwood, 30,000 gallons.
Mr. Denari has a fine place, which is situated near the Swiss-Italian Colony, on the south; a good cellar, place well improved, and vines all healthy; about 15 acres of young vineyard.

*Dotta, L., Healdsburg.*—Total, 25 acres; in wine grapes; in bearing, 20 acres; soil light gravel; valley; western exposure; crop, 50 tons; wine all sold; cooperage, redwood, 12,000 gallons.

*De Weiderhold, Mrs. A. E. S., Healdsburg.*—Total, 6 acres; all in bearing; soil light loam; upland; southern exposure; crop, 20 tons.

*Didier, J., Healdsburg.*—Total, 10 acres; all in bearing; soil red loam; mountain; northern exposure; crop, 30 tons.

*Donahue, J. M. (estate of), Littons.*—Total, 55 acres; all in bearing; soil light loam and gravelly; upland; southern exposure; crop, 85 tons.
This vineyard appears to be in a healthy condition, but has not been carefully cultivated.

*Ellis, L. G., Geyserville.*—Total, 13 acres; all in bearing; soil deep black loam; low lying; southern exposure; crop, 50 tons.
This was the first place in the valley where phylloxera made its appearance. It has been observed in this vineyard for three years past, but has been confined to two or three small spots of about an acre all told. The remainder of the vineyard appears to be healthy. Mr. Ellis has no idea as to how phylloxera got a foothold in his vineyard. He says there has been no interchange of grape boxes with any infested orchard. His place is across the river from Geyserville, in a belt of very rich country, entirely surrounded by the Russian River and high hills or mountains. It is a thoroughly protected spot, so far as contact with the outside world is concerned. At first the disease appeared but in one spot, which has increased in size each year. The next season two other spots some twenty rods distant were affected, a few vines dying at each. Mr. Ellis has put in a few resistants, with which he is experimenting.

*Elliott, John, Cloverdale.*—Total, 10 acres; all in bearing; soil alluvial; upland; crop, 30 tons.

*Elliott, J. B., Cloverdale.*—Total, 6 acres; all in bearing; soil light sandy; low lying; valley; crop, 42 tons.
.This vineyard is situated in Oat Valley, near Preston.

*Fairchild, O. G., Geyserville.*—Total, 6 acres; all in bearing; soil gravelly; upland; eastern exposure; crop, 30 tons.

*Fay, J. P., Geyserville.*—Total, 7 acres; all in bearing; soil loam; upland; crop, 15 tons.

*Fay, John H., Geyserville.*—Total, 18 acres; in wine grapes; in bearing, 15 acres; soil gravelly; low lying; exposure, protected by hills; crop, 75 tons.
Mr. Fay's place is opposite Geyserville, in Alexander Valley.

*Farmers and Merchants Bank, Healdsburg.*—Total, 12 acres; all in bearing; soil light loam; valley; southern exposure; crop, 40 tons.

*Feely, M. J., Healdsburg.*—Total, 8 acres; all in bearing; soil black loose loam; low lying; exposure, nearly level; crop, 45 tons.

*Ferguson, John N., Alexander Valley.*—Total, 26 acres; in wine grapes; in bearing, 23 acres; soil red sandy loam; upland; westerly exposure; crop, 115 tons.

*Ferguson, H. O., Healdsburg.*—Total, 10 acres; all in bearing; soil red; valley; southern exposure; crop, 30 tons.

*Ferguson, P. J., Healdsburg.*—Total, 8 acres; all in bearing; soil gravelly loam; upland; westerly exposure; crop, 35 tons from these 8 acres; had 18 acres last year, with a crop of 65 tons; sold 10 acres since last vintage.

*Folkers, J. H. A., Kellogg.*—Total, 60 acres; all in bearing; resistants, 40 acres; Riparia, 10 acres; Lenoir, 30 acres; grafted and in bearing, 40 acres; not yet grafted, 2 acres; varieties succeeding best: Semillon on Riparia, French on Lenoir; soil black loam interspersed with gravel, and decomposed rock; upland and mountain side; southwest and south exposure; crop, 200 tons.

*Foster, William E., Healdsburg.*—Total, 18 acres; in wine grapes, 16 acres; in table grapes, 2 acres; soil gravelly; upland; exposure, level, fully exposed to both sun and wind; crop, 70 tons.

*Frank, D. C., Healdsburg.*—Total, 5 acres; all in bearing; soil light loam; valley; southern exposure; crop, 15 tons.

*Frampton, Mrs., Healdsburg.*—Total, 20 acres; in wine grapes; in bearing, 15 acres; soil light loam; upland; western exposure; crop, 25 tons.
This vineyard is at the base of Fitch Mountain, north of Healdsburg.

*Fricke & Priest, Cozzens.*—Total, 20 acres; all in bearing; soil red; valley; southern exposure; crop, 70 tons; wine all sold; cooperage, 30,000 gallons.

*Furber, E. G., Cloverdale.*—Total, 50 acres; all in bearing; soil red; hilly; southern exposure; crop, 200 tons; cooperage, oak, 20,000 gallons; redwood, 20,000 gallons.
A good vineyard, adjoining hills on west side of Russian River Valley; cellar and small distillery.

*Frei, L., & Co., San Francisco.*—Total, 135 acres; in wine grapes; in bearing, 125 acres; soil red and light gravelly; upland; southern exposure; crop, 400 tons; wine all sold; cooperage, redwood, 50,000 gallons.

*Ferry, John, Cloverdale.*—Total, 18 acres; in wine grapes, 16 acres; in table grapes, 2 acres; soil red clay and gravelly; mountain; south and west exposure; crop, 40 tons.

*Galloway Bros., Healdsburg.*—Total, 57 acres; in wine grapes, 41 acres; in table grapes, 16 acres; soil black gravelly and loam; 50 acres upland, 7 acres bottom; exposure, level; crop, 235 tons of wine grapes and 30 tons of table grapes; cooperage, redwood, 20,000 gallons.
Do not think they have any phylloxera, but am not sure.

*Gardner, J., Cloverdale.*—Total, 6 acres; all in bearing; soil, hillside, black gravelly; upland; westerly exposure; crop, 8 tons.

*Gardini, John, Healdsburg.*—Total, 50 acres; all in bearing; soil light gravelly loam; mountain; south and west exposure; crop, 100 tons.

*Gater, J. E., Geyserville.*—Total, 20 acres; all in bearing; soil gravelly; upland; eastern exposure; crop, 40 tons.
This vineyard is on the west side of Russian River. Wine cellar burned down a year or two ago.

*Gibbons, Isaac, Cloverdale.*—Total, 18 acres; all in bearing; soil light gravelly; upland; exposure south and west; crop, 70 tons.
Situated at base of mountains on east side of Russian River and opposite Asti.

*Gibney, George, Geyserville.*—Total, 13 acres; all in bearing; soil light loam; valley; exposure east and south; crop, 25 tons.

*Ginnochio, Mrs. G., Asti.*—Total, 100 acres; all in bearing; soil light gravelly; upland; southern exposure; crop, 150 tons.

*Gird, H. S., Alexander Valley.*—Total, 6 acres; all in bearing; soil light gravelly; upland; southern exposure; crop, 15 tons.

*Goetzelman, J., Cloverdale.*—Total, 8 acres; all in bearing; soil light gravelly; upland; southern exposure; crop, 25 tons.

*Goddard, Daniel, Healdsburg.*—Total, 15 acres; all in bearing; soil red gravelly loam; upland; southern exposure; crop, 30 tons.

*Goodrich, W., Alexander Valley.*—Total, 19 acres; all in bearing; soil gravelly; valley; southern exposure; crop, 80 tons.

*Gum, I., Healdsburg.*—Total, 20 acres; all in bearing; soil red loam; upland; northwestern exposure; crop, 31 tons.
A small crop last year, on account of not having been properly taken care of and cultivated. This vineyard will average 50 tons per annum, one year with another.

*Haehl, C., Cloverdale.*—Total, 20 acres; in wine grapes; in bearing, 18 acres; soil gravelly loam, with clay subsoil; upland; eastern exposure; crop, 60 tons; very little wine on hand; cooperage, oak, 10,000 gallons; redwood, 10,000 gallons.

*Hagmayer, G., Cloverdale.*—Total, 6 acres; in wine grapes, 4 acres; in table grapes, 1 acre; in raisin grapes, 1 acre; soil red; upland; southern exposure; crop, 20 tons. Has planted olives in his vineyard this year.

*Haigh, E., Littons.*—Total, 5 acres; all in bearing; soil gravelly; valley; eastern exposure; crop, 15 tons.

*Hale, M. M., Geyserville.*—Total, 17 acres; in wine grapes; in bearing, 16 acres; soil gravelly loam; three fourths low lying, remainder hilly; exposure, slopes to the south; crop, 41 tons.

*Hall, B. W., Cloverdale.*—Total, 25 acres; in wine grapes; in bearing, 18 acres; soil light sandy; low lying; exposure, level, full; crop, 100 tons.

*Hall, L., & Son, Littons.*—Total, 25 acres; all in bearing; soil light loam; valley; southern exposure; crop, 50 tons.

*Hall, D. W., Cloverdale.*—Total, 30 acres; in wine grapes; in bearing, 23 acres; soil light loam; valley; western exposure; crop, 75 tons.
A good, healthy vineyard, on the east side of the Russian River, 7 acres being young vines, and expects to set out about 20 or 30 acres more next season.

*Hallengren, S. P., Geyserville.*—Total, 20 acres; all in bearing; seven years old; soil gravelly and clay; upland; exposure, direct; crop, 50 tons, this being first crop.

*Hamilton, G. S., Healdsburg.*—Total, 25 acres; all in bearing; soil gravelly; table and hill land; exposure, all directions; crop, 60 tons.
A few Zinfandel vines appear sickly, but the disease is not known to be phylloxera.

*Hammekin, Henry, Healdsburg.*—Total, 11 acres; in wine grapes; in bearing, 9 acres; soil gravelly; part low lying and part upland; crop, 26 tons.

*Heald, J. G., Cloverdale.*—Total, 38 acres; all in bearing; soil light loam; valley; exposure north and east; crop, 213 tons.

*Heaton, G. O., Healdsburg.*—Total, 20 acres; all in bearing; soil light loam; valley; southern exposure; crop, 80 tons.

*Heinicke, Mrs., Alexander Valley.*—Total, 7 acres; all in bearing; soil light gravelly; mountain; southerly exposure; crop, 15 tons.

*Hendricks, J., Healdsburg.*—Total, 14 acres; all in bearing; soil black gravelly; low lying; southwesterly exposure; crop, 84 tons.

*Hermann, Mrs., Cloverdale.*—Total, 20 acres; all in bearing; soil light loam; valley; southern exposure; crop, 50 tons.

*Higgs, Mrs. Mary, Cozzens.*—Total, 20 acres; all in bearing; soil light gravelly; upland; southern exposure; crop, 50 tons.

*Hilberrer, Philip, Geyserville.*—Total, 7 acres; all in bearing; soil light gravelly; upland; eastern exposure; crop, 30 tons.

*Hill, F. S., Healdsburg.*—Total, 10 acres; all in bearing; soil red; upland; southern exposure; crop, 25 tons.

*Hixon, James, Cloverdale.*—Total, 6 acres; all in bearing; soil light loam; valley; western exposure; crop, 15 tons.

*Hoadly, Mrs. I. T., Cloverdale.*—Total, 8 acres; all in bearing; soil red and black gravelly, low lying and part hill; crop, 30 tons.

*Hodges, H. C., Healdsburg.*—Total, 16 acres; all in bearing; soil clay loam; upland; exposure, south hillside; crop, 40 tons.

*Holloway, J. C., Cloverdale.*—Total, 62 acres; all in bearing; soil gravelly loam; upland; exposure, all directions; crop, 150 tons.

*Holmes, C. H., Kellogg.*—Total, 10 acres; all in bearing; soil gravelly loam; upland; crop, 30 tons.

*Holst, Peter N., Healdsburg.*—Total, 40 acres; in wine grapes; in bearing, 35 acres; soil mixed; upland; crop, 80 tons; cooperage, oak, 2,000 gallons; redwood, 23,000 gallons.

*Hood, George, Santa Rosa.*—Vineyard in Knights Valley, near Kellogg Post Office. Total, 93 acres; planted to resistants as an experiment, there being no phylloxera in the vineyard; soil red gravel and sandy loam; upland; rolling hills, facing all directions; crop in 1892, about 200 tons, from which 30,000 gallons of wine were made; stock of wine on hand, 35,000 gallons; cooperage, 60,000 gallons, of which 40,000 gallons is oak and 20,000 gallons is redwood.

*Hopkins, M. (estate of), Healdsburg.*—Total, 240 acres; all in bearing; soil red, a light gravelly loam; mountain and upland; southern exposure; crop, 600 tons.
This is one of the largest vineyards in the county, and is situated in hills on the north side of Russian River. Vines all healthy.

*Howard, S. D., Cloverdale.*—Total, 25 acres; all in bearing; soil black loam; upland; exposure south and east; crop, 50 tons.

*Howland & Wheldon, Healdsburg.*—Total, 10 acres; all in bearing; soil light gravel; upland; southern exposure; crop, 20 tons.

*Italian-Swiss Agricultural Colony, Asti.*—Total, 650 acres; in wine grapes; in bearing, 600 acres; hillsides; crop, two thirds; cooperage, oak, 150,000 gallons; redwood, 850,000 gallons.

A number of vines have died on this place, but the management insists that there is no phylloxera on the place.

*Isaacs, Andrew, Healdsburg.*—Total, 7 acres; in wine grapes, 6 acres; in table grapes, 1 acre; soil clay; upland; exposure south and east; crop, 15 tons.

*Jaffe, L., Healdsburg.*—Total, 15 acres; all in bearing; soil red; mountain; exposure east and north; crop, 50 tons; cooperage, redwood, 20,000 gallons.

*Jehle, Leo, Healdsburg.*—Total, 12 acres; all in bearing; soil clay loam; upland; crop, 24 tons.

*Jewett, D. G., Healdsburg.*—Total, 6 acres; all in bearing; soil part clay, balance gravelly loam; upland; crop, 20 tons.

*Jones, B. M., Littons.*—Total, 15 acres; all in bearing; soil light sandy soil; valley; southern exposure; crop, 40 tons.

*Kayser, A. H., Soda Rock.*—Total, 5 acres; all in bearing; soil clay loam; upland; crop, 5 tons.

Mr. Kayser will take up his vines and plant the ground to something else.

*Kellogg, Mrs., Cozzens.*—Total, 20 acres; all in bearing; soil light gravelly; valley; southern exposure; crop, 90 tons.

*Kind, William, Healdsburg.*—Total, 10 acres; all in bearing; soil light gravelly loam; upland; southern exposure; crop, 25 tons.

*King, John, Healdsburg.*—Total, 44 acres; in wine grapes, 42 acres; in table grapes, 2 acres; soil red; all rolling land; northerly exposure; crop, 75 tons.

*Lane, R. J., Healdsburg.*—Total, 6 acres; in wine grapes, 3 acres; in table grapes, 3 acres; soil red clay; upland; southeast exposure; crop, 12 tons.

*Laughlin, M., Healdsburg.*—Total, 10 acres; all in bearing; soil light loam; upland; southern exposure; crop, 25 tons.

*Laughlin, Mrs. E., Healdsburg.*—Total, 10 acres; all in bearing; soil light gravelly loam; upland; southern exposure; crop, 20 tons.

*Larison, Samuel, Preston.*—Total, 25 acres; all in bearing; soil red gravelly; upland; eastern exposure; crop, 50 tons.

*Leger, A. C., Cloverdale.*—Total, 12 acres; in wine grapes; in bearing, 10 acres; soil gravelly; low lying; southerly exposure; crop, 25 tons.

*Lee, ——, Alexander Valley* (lives at Colusa).—Total, 12 acres; all in bearing; soil alluvial; low lying; crop, 25 tons.

*Leroux, Jule, Cloverdale.*—Total, 16 acres; all in bearing; soil light gravelly; upland; eastern exposure; crop, 50 tons; cooperage, 3,000 gallons in oak, 15,000 in redwood.

*Leroux, Peter, Cloverdale.*—Total, 20 acres; all in bearing; soil light loam; valley; exposure south and east; crop, 60 tons.

Mr. Leroux's vineyard is situated near the Swiss-Italian Colony.

*Lewis, R. E., Healdsburg.*—Total, 70 acres; in wine grapes, 65 acres; in table grapes, 5 acres; soil gravelly loam; upland; southeasterly exposure; crop, 230 tons.

*Lewis, R. M., Healdsburg.*—Total, 5 acres; all in bearing; soil light loam; upland; southern exposure; crop, 15 tons.

*Liter, J. L., Healdsburg.*—Total, 7 acres; all in bearing; soil light loam; valley; southern exposure; crop, 15 tons.

*Llewellyn & Co., William, Cloverdale.*—Total, 50 acres; all in bearing; soil gravelly; mountain; exposure south and east; crop, 100 tons.

*Long, Isaac, Littons.*—Total, 60 acres; all in bearing; soil light gravelly; low lying; exposure east and south; crop, 156 tons.

*Lombardy, Severino, Healdsburg.*—Total, 5 acres; all in bearing; soil light; upland; southern exposure; crop, 15 tons.

*Luken, H. B., Healdsburg.*—Total, 10 acres; all in bearing; soil light and stony; steep hills; exposure, all directions; crop, 25 tons.

*Mack, William, Soda Rock.*—Total, 22 acres; all in bearing; soil red; valley; western exposure; crop, 4 tons.
This is a young vineyard recently set out on the south side of Alexander Valley.

*Masona & Scatena, Healdsburg.*—Total, 60 acres; all in bearing; soil light gravelly; upland; southern exposure; crop, 200 tons; wine on hand, 8,000 gallons; cooperage, redwood, 30,000 gallons.

*Matthews, Charles, Alexander Valley.*—Total, 7 acres; all in bearing; soil light gravelly; valley; northern exposure; crop, 25 tons.

*Matthews, John W., Alexander Valley.*—Total, 10 acres; all in bearing; soil light gravelly; low lying; northern exposure; crop, 30 tons.

*Matthews, Wesley, Alexander Valley.*—Total, 30 acres; all in bearing; soil red; valley; northern exposure; crop, 100 tons.
This vineyard is on the south side of Russian River.

*McCarthy, William, Healdsburg.*—Total, 5 acres; all in bearing; soil light gravelly; valley; south and east exposure; crop, 10 tons.

*McLaughlin, C. W., Healdsburg.*—Total, 10 acres; all in bearing; soil reddish alluvial; hillside and slope; exposure, varied; crop, 20 tons.
There are no signs of mildew or phylloxera, nor of any other disease of vine or fruit. Sugar test is high and yield light, as compared with valley vineyards.

*McClish, John, Healdsburg.*—Total, 13 acres; all in bearing; soil gravelly; upland; crop, 60 tons.

*McCray, W. H., Cloverdale.*—Total, 20 acres; all in bearing; soil black loam; upland; exposure south and east; crop, 40 tons.

*McDonald, Frank, Calistoga.*—Total, 8 acres; in wine grapes, 5 acres; in table grapes, 2 acres; in raisin grapes, 1 acre; soil red hill land; on a sidehill; easterly exposure; crop, 6 tons.

*McDonough, Michael, Geyserville.*—Total, 13 acres; all in bearing; soil light gravelly; valley and mountain; eastern exposure; crop, 50 tons.

*McElarney (estate) & Smith, Cloverdale.*—Total, 40 acres; in wine grapes; in bearing, 26 acres; soil red; valley; western and southern exposure; crop, 75 tons; wine on hand, 14,000 gallons; cooperage, redwood, 20,000 gallons.
There are about 12 acres planted in young vines. The vineyard is healthy, and is in the center of the Russian River Valley.

*Merchant, T. S., Healdsburg.*—Total, 160 acres; all in bearing; soil red gravelly; mountain; southern exposure; crop, 300 tons.
The vineyard is in hills on the north side of Russian River; vines healthy and looking well.

*Meyer, Claus, Geyserville.*—Total, 25 acres; all in bearing; soil light gravelly; valley; southern exposure; crop, 160 tons.

*Meyer, Henry, Geyserville.*—Total, 15 acres; all in bearing; soil light gravelly; valley; southern exposure; crop, 100 tons.
The Zinfandel on this place reported as yielding 10 tons to the acre.

*Meyer, John, Healdsburg.*—Total, 15 acres; all in bearing; soil red; upland; exposure north; crop, 20 tons.

*Meyerholtz, Henry, Petaluma.*—Total, 20 acres; all in bearing; soil light gravelly; upland; southern exposure; crop, 75 tons.
This vineyard is situated at base of hills on east side of Russian River.

*Michaelsen Bros., Alexander Valley.*—Total, 25 acres; all in bearing, and all wine grapes; red soil; upland; southern exposure; crop, 60 tons; stock of wine on hand, 7,000 gallons; cooperage, 10,000 gallons, all oak.

*Miller, James, Healdsburg.*—Total, 25 acres; all in bearing; soil light loam; upland; southern exposure; crop, 100 tons.
This vineyard is at entrance to Dry Creek Valley, and is a productive place.

*Minari, Thomas, Geyserville.*—Total, 10 acres; all in bearing; soil black loam; valley; southern exposure; crop, 20 tons.

*More, C. P., Geyscrville.*—Total, 20 acres; all in bearing; soil light sandy loam; valley; south and east exposure; crop, 40 tons.
This vineyard is affected to some extent by phylloxera, which was first discovered about two years ago, and is supposed to have been brought here in grape boxes from Sonoma Valley. Nothing has been done in the way of treatment of the vineyard for the disease.

*Moreland, W. W., Healdsburg.*—Total, 6 acres; all in bearing; soil red loam; mountain; southern exposure; crop, 20 tons.

*Morrill, Mrs. F. A., Geyserville.*—Total, 10 acres; in wine grapes, 8 acres; in table grapes, 2 acres; soil dark loam; valley; southern exposure; crop, 30 tons.

*Morisoli, M., Healdsburg.*—Total, 15 acres; all in bearing; soil red; mountain; southern exposure; crop, 30 tons.

*Mothorn, William, Healdsburg.*—Total, 15 acres; all in bearing; soil red; upland; southern exposure; crop, 50 tons.

*Mowbray, Mrs., Preston.*—Total, 10 acres; all in bearing; soil red; valley; eastern exposure; crop, 30 tons.

*Moulton, A. W., San Francisco* (F. Albertz, lessee, Cloverdale).—Total, 72 acres; in wine grapes, 70 acres; in table grapes, 2 acres; soil red loam; upland; crop, 175 tons; wine on hand, 10,000 gallons; cooperage, oak, 20,000; redwood, 125,000 gallons.
Three acres of Riparia roots will be planted, also one half acre of Lenoir, this season.

*Mulcahey, J., Alexander Valley.*—Total, 10 acres; all in bearing; soil red; mountain; southern exposure; crop, 30 tons.

*Neery, M., "Whitcomb Place," Healdsburg.*—Total, 12 acres; all in bearing; crop, 30 tons.

*Newcom, H., Cozzens.*—Total, 10 acres; all in bearing; soil light loam; valley; southern exposure; crop, 40 tons.

*Norton, E. M., Healdsburg.*—Total, 100 acres; all in bearing; soil lies in separate tracts, 60 acres in hills and 40 acres river bottom; hill land is light, gravelly, and limey; 30 acres on Mill Creek, partly shaded and sheltered, balance exposed; crop, 250 tons; cooperage, redwood, 12,000 gallons.

*Ottmer, H. C., Healdsburg.*—Total, 18 acres; all in bearing; soil gravelly and creek bottom; upland; exposure full; crop, 110 tons.

*Ogilvie, Captain, Healdsburg.*—Total, 6 acres; all in bearing; soil light gravelly; upland; southern exposure; crop, 15 tons.

*Ormsby, M. P., Geyserville.*—Total, 5 acres; all in bearing; soil red loam; upland; exposure southeast; crop, 15 tons.
Mr. Ormsby has dug up all of his vineyard excepting 5 acres, and has planted the ground to fruit, which he finds more profitable. The remainder of his vineyard has been planted to fruit trees, and as soon as they are in bearing the vines will be taken out.

*Osborn, S. L., Alexander Valley.*—Total, 140 acres; all in bearing; soil red and black loam; upland; exposure southeast; crop, 400 tons.
This is a very fine appearing vineyard; the vines have been properly cared for and they are strong, vigorous growers and good bearers.

*Parker Vineyard Co., Cloverdale.*—Total, 40 acres; in wine grapes; in bearing, 30 acres; soil red gravelly; mountain; rolling hills, giving both north and south exposure; crop, 37 tons; wine on hand, 7,000 gallons; cooperage, oak, 3,000 gallons; redwood, 15,000 gallons.
About 10 acres of young vines have been set out on this place; vines are looking healthy and no indication of disease of any kind.

*Parker, Isaac, Healdsburg.*—Total, 16 acres; in wine grapes; in bearing, 12 acres; soil, part rich bottom, part red land; part bottom and part upland; exposure, level land, no protection from wind; crop, 70 tons.
The upland portion of the vineyard bears better than on the creek bottom.

*Parsons, I. N., Santa Rosa.*—Vineyard across Russian River, east of Geyserville. Total, 10 acres; all in bearing; soil light gravelly; upland and valley; western exposure; crop, 20 tons.

*Parsons, Thos., Cloverdale.*—Total, 5 acres; all in bearing; soil gravelly; mountain; southern exposure; crop, 10 tons.

*Parkerson, C. J., Healdsburg.*—Total, 10 acres; all in bearing; soil black; valley; northern exposure; crop, 20 tons.

*Passalaqua, A. B., Healdsburg.*—Total, 17 acres; all in bearing; soil black and red loam; valley and mountain; exposure south and east; crop, 60 tons.
A prolific vineyard, partly in bottom land and partly on hills, west of Healdsburg.

*Patton, R. R., Cozzens.*—Total, 6 acres; all in bearing; soil light loam; valley; exposure north and east; crop, 20 tons.

*Patronack, F. F., Grass Valley.*—This vineyard is on Dry Creek, north of Healdsburg. Total, 20 acres; all in bearing; soil black loam; valley; northern exposure; crop, 150 tons; cooperage, redwood, 45,000 gallons.

*Patterson, Solomon, Healdsburg.*—Total, 16 acres; all in bearing; soil gravelly; upland; southern exposure; crop, 40 tons.

*Patten, F., Healdsburg.*—Total, 30 acres; all in bearing; soil black loam; valley; southern exposure; crop, 130 tons.

*Paxton, Mrs. J. A., Healdsburg.*—Total, 90 acres; all in bearing; soiľred loam; mountain; eastern exposure; crop, 180 tons; cooperage, oak, 35,000 gallons; redwood, 35,000 gallons. A good vineyard, on hills west of Healdsburg; fine large stone wine cellar; vines healthy.

*Plumb, William, Healdsburg.*—Total, 10 acres; all in bearing; soil light gravelly; upland; southern exposure; crop, 20 tons.

*Powell, R., Healdsburg.*—Total, 6 acres; all in bearing; soil light loam; upland; southern exposure; crop, 10 tons.

*Peterson, Carl L. F., Geyserville.*—Total, 5 acres; all in bearing; soil mellow black; low lying; crop, 18 tons; no disease.

*Perazzo, G., Asti.*—Total, 27 acres; all in bearing; soil gravelly; upland; southern exposure; crop, 100 tons.

*Petray, George W., Geyserville.*—Total, 7 acres; all in bearing; soil light loam; valley; southern exposure; crop, 18 tons.

*Phillips, D. D., Healdsburg.*—Total, 45 acres; in wine grapes, 44 acres; in table grapes, ½ acre; in raisin grapes, ½ acre; good deep soil; low lying; exposure, comparatively level; crop, 150 tons.

*Phillips, Mrs L., Cozzens.*—Total, 11 acres; all in bearing; soil light; valley; exposure north and east; crop, 40 tons.

*Plaskett, Peter, Cloverdale.*—Total, 5 acres; all in bearing; soil light loam; valley; eastern exposure; crop, 15 tons.

*Pohley, F., Windsor.*—Total, 30 acres; in wine grapes; in bearing, 20 acres; soil red loam; hilly; northern exposure; crop, 70 tons; mostly new vineyard, and has recently changed hands.

*Porterfield, W. H., Cloverdale.*—Total, 30 acres; all in bearing; soil red; valley; exposure south; crop, 100 tons.

*Portupita, I. W., Cloverdale.*—Total, 28 acres; in wine grapes, 25 acres; in raisin grapes, 3 acres; soil red; upland; exposure, all directions; crop, 145 tons wine grapes, 10 tons Muscats.

*Preston, Mrs. E., Preston.*—Total, 8 acres; all in bearing; mountain; exposure west; crop, 30 tons; wine on hand, 40,000 gallons; cooperage, oak, 8,000 gallons.

*Price, John, Cozzens.*—Total, 15 acres; all in bearing; soil light loam; valley; exposure south; crop, 50 tons.

*Pritchett, M., Cozzens.*—Total, 10 acres; all in bearing; soil light gravelly; valley; southern exposure; crop, 45 tons.

*Prouse, Daniel, Healdsburg.*—Total, 20 acres; all in bearing; soil red; upland; northern exposure; crop, 70 tons.

*Prows, Sylvester, Healdsburg.*—Total, 25 acres; all in bearing; soil red gravelly; mountain; eastern exposure; crop, 40 tons.

*Puccerido, C., Cloverdale.*—Total, 25 acres; all in bearing; soil gravelly; upland; southern exposure; crop, 70 tons.

*Purser, Edward Thomas, Healdsburg.*—Total, 20 acres; in bearing, 18 acres; soil red hilly; rolling upland; exposure south and west; crop, 51 tons.

*Radskey, Fred. W., Cloverdale.*—Total, 9 acres; all in bearing; soil gravelly; upland; southern exposure; crop, 45 tons.

*Rafael, Angelo, Geyserville.*—Total, 25 acres; all in bearing; soil gravelly; mountain; eastern exposure; crop, 50 tons.
This vineyard is on a mountain west of Geyserville.

*Redington & Co., San Francisco.*—Total, 85 acres; all in bearing; soil light loam; valley and mountain; eastern and southern exposure; crop, 120 tons.
A part of the C. P. Moore place, now worked by the Italian-Swiss Colony. There are indications of disease in this vineyard; whether phylloxera or not is not determined.

*Reiners, C. A., Healdsburg.*—Total, 70 acres; in wine grapes; in bearing, 40 acres; soil chocolate loam; upland; crop, 100 tons; wine on hand, 13,000 gallons; cooperage, 40,000 gallons, of which 10,000 gallons is oak and 30,000 gallons is redwood; vintage of 1892 made 30,000 gallons of wine and 2,000 gallons of brandy.

*Reniff, A. A., Geyserville.*—Total, 10 acres; in wine grapes, 9 acres; in table grapes, 1 acre; soil red; upland; exposure south and east; crop, 1 ton.

*Rickman, H., Healdsburg.*—Total, 12 acres; all in bearing; soil light gravelly; mountain; eastern exposure; crop, 30 tons.

*Robinson, H., Healdsburg.*—Total, 15 acres; all in bearing; soil red; mountain; west and south exposure; crop, 40 tons.

*Robinson, J., Healdsburg.*—Total, 5 acres; all in bearing; soil red; valley; west exposure; crop, 20 tons.

*Rogers, John L., Healdsburg.*—Total, 16 acres; in wine grapes, 14 acres; in table grapes, 2 acres; soil, half dark gravelly and half red; southern exposure; crop, 90 tons.

*Ross, R. B., Healdsburg.*—Total, 8 acres; all in bearing; soil light loam; upland; exposure west and south; crop, 20 tons.

*Rose, F., Healdsburg.*—Total, 6 acres; all in bearing; soil light loam; upland; southern exposure; crop, 16 tons.

*Routtkey, F. W., Cloverdale.*—Total, 7 acres; all in bearing; soil gravelly loam; upland; crop, 48½ tons.

*Runnel, Mrs. Chas., Geyserville.*—Total, 2½ acres; all in bearing; soil light gravelly; upland; eastern exposure; crop, 15 tons.

*Sarcinsson, C., Healdsburg.*—Total, 8 acres; in wine grapes, 7 acres; in raisin grapes, 1 acre; soil red gravelly; upland; southern exposure; cooperage, redwood, 2,000 gallons.

*Saum, George, Healdsburg.*—Total, 5 acres; all in bearing; soil red; upland; southern exposure; crop, 15 tons.

*Savier, N. J., Cloverdale.*—Total, 8 acres; in bearing, 6 acres; wine grapes; soil red; mountain; southern exposure; crop, 16 tons.

*Scioali, V., Healdsburg.*—Total, 8 acres; all in bearing; soil red loam; mountain; southern exposure; crop, 30 tons.

*Schwartz & Cohn, San Francisco* (vineyard in Alameda Valley).—Total, 80 acres; all in bearing; soil light gravelly; valley; southern exposure; crop, 300 tons.

*Schnitzger, C. H., Geyserville.*—Total, 20 acres; all in bearing; soil light gravelly; valley; southern exposure; crop, 80 tons.

*Semple, C. E., Cloverdale.*—Total, 5 acres; all in bearing; soil gravelly; mountain; southern exposure: crop, 10 tons.

*Shearer, Mrs., Healdsburg.*—Total, 5 acres; all in bearing; soil light loam; upland; southern exposure; crop, 10 tons.

*Shanks, Dr. (estate of).*—Total, 15 acres; all in bearing; soil gravelly; mountain; western exposure; crop, 30 tons.

*Simi, P. & G., Healdsburg.*—Total, 126 acres; all in bearing; soil light sandy; upland; southern exposure; crop, 300 tons; wine on hand, 150,000 gallons; cooperage, 200,000 gallons.
This is a large vineyard just north of Healdsburg; healthy vines and a large new stone wine cellar.

*Sink, D. & W. D., Cloverdale.*—Total, 50 acres; all in bearing; soil light loam; valley; eastern exposure; crop, 175 tons.

*Smith, W. T., Geyserville.*—Total, 55 acres; all in bearing; soil black gravelly; 35 acres valley and remainder upland; crop, 200 tons.

*Snook, Mrs., Healdsburg.*—Total, 11 acres; all in bearing; soil red; upland; exposure west and south; crop, 30 tons.

*Snider, Mrs. J., Healdsburg.*—Total, 13 acres; all in bearing; soil light; valley; exposure south; crop, 60 tons.

*Southern, Mrs., Cloverdale.*—Total, 14 acres; all in bearing; soil light loam; valley; exposure south and west; crop, 35 tons.

*Steinbach, Fred., Healdsburg.*—Total, 10 acres; in wine grapes; in bearing, 6 acres; soil light gravelly; mountain; western exposure; crop, 15 tons.

*Stiode, S. E., Geyserville.*—Total, 14 acres; all in bearing; soil sandy loam, some clay; low lying; crop, 65 tons.

*Story, George, Healdsburg.*—Total, 6 acres; all in bearing; soil gravelly loam; upland; eastern exposure; crop, 15 tons.

*Stamer & Feldmeyer, Geyserville.*—Total, 37 acres; all in bearing; soil mostly gravelly, hill slate, clay; valley and upland; hilly about 5 acres; northern exposure; crop, on 27 acres, 85 tons; cooperage, oak, 25,000 puncheons; redwood, 50,000 puncheons; 10 acres of vineyard only lately acquired by present owner; crop, about 28 tons.

*Strode, Charles.*—Total, 8 acres; all in bearing; soil light gravelly; valley; southern exposure; crop, 25 tons.

*Stewart, Fred. W., Geyserville.*—Total, 15 acres; all in bearing; soil red; mountain; southern exposure; crop, 40 tons.

*Stites, A. H., Geyserville.*—Total, 12 acres; in wine grapes, 11 acres; in table grapes, 1 acre; soil, part gravelly, part clay; low lying; exposure direct, being nearly all level land; crop, 35 tons.

*Sylvester, Harlan & Co., Geyserville.*—Total, 38 acres; all in bearing; soil sandy loam; valley; eastern exposure; crop, 200 tons.

*Teaby, W. H., Geyserville.*—Total, 10 acres; all in bearing; made soil; crop, 18 tons.

*Templeton, John, Healdsburg.*—Total, 8 acres; all in bearing; soil light gravelly; upland; southern exposure; crop, 20 tons.

*Thomsen Bros., Cozzens.*—Total, 15 acres; in wine grapes; in bearing, 13 acres; soil black, and red gravelly clay; upland and mountain; southerly exposure; crop, 45 tons; wine on hand, 10,000 gallons, all sold but not delivered; cooperage, oak, 1,500 gallons; redwood, 12,000 gallons.
No phylloxera found. A few Lenoir planted experimentally, scattered through vineyard, grafted to Crabb's Burgundy, Mataro, and Sweetwater; Mataro succeeds best. Are commencing experiments with Riparia and Rupestris.

*Thormann, A., Alexander Valley.*—Total, 25 acres; all in bearing; crop, 100 tons.

*Todd, P. W., Santa Rosa.*—The vineyard is near Cloverdale. Total, 20 acres; all in bearing and all wine grapes; soil light loam; low lying; eastern exposure; crop, 90 tons.

*Treadway, D. G., Healdsburg.*—Total, 25 acres; all in bearing; red and black loam; upland; northern exposure; crop, 100 tons.

*Trapet. J. B., Healdsburg.*—Total, 16 acres; in bearing, 15 acres; soil black loam, with red gravel below; upland; crop, 60 tons; made 8,600 gallons of wine; cooperage, oak, 2,000 gallons; redwood, 13,000 gallons.

*Truitt, Mrs., Healdsburg.*—Total, 6 acres; all in bearing; soil light loam; upland; eastern exposure; crop, 15 tons.

*Tucker, John, Healdsburg.*—Total, 30 acres; all in bearing; soil light gravelly loam; upland; southern exposure; crop, 75 tons.

*Turner, John H., Cloverdale.*—Total, 10 acres; all in bearing; soil sandy loam; low lying; exposure direct to sun and wind; crop, 10 tons.
Mr. Turner writes that his crop is very light. Grapes do not seem to do well on the bottom land; they either sunburn, mildew, or rot; the gravelly lands are best for grapes.

*Van Allen, William, Healdsburg.*—Total, 21 acres; all in bearing; soil sandy loam; low lying; level; crop, 100 tons.

*Wageler, Mrs., Cozzens.*—Total, 22 acres; all in bearing; soil light loam; valley; southern exposure; crop, 100 tons.

*Walden Company (limited), Geyserville.*—Total, 40 acres; in wine grapes; in bearing, 30 acres; soil black loam and gravel, varies; part lowland and part upland; exposure south and east; crop, 15 tons; cooperage, redwood, 300,000 gallons.

*Walker, B. F., Cozzens.*—Total, 6 acres; all in bearing; soil light loam; upland; exposure south and east; crop, 20 tons.

*Wambold, D. M., Cloverdale.*—Total, 4 acres; all in bearing; soil gravelly; low lying; crop, 8 tons.
A late hail storm seriously damaged the crop in 1892; the same patch produced about 20 tons in 1891, and about 40 tons in 1890.

*Warren, W. P., Alexander Valley.*—Total, 17 acres; in wine grapes; in bearing, 16 acres; soil red loam; exposure, gentle slope to the east; crop, 63 tons.
Mr. Warren says: "I have no resistant or grafted vines. My vineyard consists of Burger, Malvoisie, Zinfandel, Firisago, and Carignan, about equally divided. I like the Burger and Carignan best; the Malvoisie is a good bearer and is profitable to raise for brandy."

*Warner, A. L., Healdsburg.*—Total, 22 acres; in wine grapes, 20 acres; in table grapes, 2 acres; have set out trees on about 12 acres, by taking out every third vine in every third row; a very little phylloxera has just made its appearance in one or two places; soil mostly of a black gravelly loam; upland; rather sheltered from the northwest wind, but fair to the sun; crop, 100 tons.
Mr. Warner has set trees in his vineyard, thinking it a better plan to start a new vineyard with resistant vines, providing the outlook will warrant it. Thus, he taxes but very few grapes while getting the trees, and he thinks very little of trying to patch up a phylloxera vineyard.

*Warner, J. E., Healdsburg.*—Total, 11 acres; all in bearing; soil gravelly; upland; direct exposure to both sun and wind; crop, 75 tons.

*Walters, Solomon, Healdsburg.*—Total, 18 acres; all in bearing; soil red loam; upland; southern exposure; crop, 50 tons.

*Weidland, Frank, Healdsburg.*—Total, 15 acres; all in bearing; soil light gravelly; upland; southern exposure; crop, 50 tons.

*Wheaton, John, Healdsburg.*—Total, 20 acres; all in bearing; soil red; upland; southern exposure; crop, 70 tons.

*Whitney, William, Healdsburg.*—Total, 12 acres; all in bearing; soil red loam; mountain; northern exposure; crop, 40 tons.

*Wines, W. F., Santa Rosa* (winery near Soda Rock).—Total, 5 acres; all in bearing and all wine grapes; soil black loam; southern exposure; crop, 6 tons.

*Winder, Mrs. M. A., Geyserville.*—Total, 35 acres; all in bearing; soil light gravelly; upland; southern exposure; crop, 68 tons.

, *Wisecarner Estate, Geyserville.*—Total, 50 acres; all in bearing; soil sandy loam; valley; eastern and southern exposure; crop, 270 tons.

*Wise, Mrs. Marion, San Rafael.*—Vineyard on hills west of Healdsburg. Total, 50 acres; all in bearing; soil red loam; eastern exposure; crop, 60 tons; wine on hand, 4,000 gallons; cooperage, oak, 20,000 gallons; redwood, 30,000 gallons.

*Woods, J. B., Cloverdale.*—Total, 5 acres; all in bearing; soil light loam; valley; southern exposure; crop, 15 tons.

*Worth, C., Preston.*—Total, 6 acres; all in bearing; soil light loam; valley; western exposure; crop, 15 tons.

*Wright, B. F., Cozzens.*—Total, 12 acres; all in bearing; soil gravelly; upland; crop, 60 tons.

*Wrightson, Francis, Santa Rosa.*—The "Knust" Vineyard, near Cloverdale. Total, 30 acres; all in bearing; soil red gravelly; valley; western exposure; crop, 70 tons.

*Yordi, Fred., Cloverdale.*—Total, 17 acres; all in bearing; soil red; crop, 50 tons. Mr. Yordi has not discovered any phylloxera as yet; vineyard mostly Zinfandel.

*Young & Hobbs, Alexander Valley.*—Total, 22 acres; all in bearing; soil red; valley; western exposure; crop, 40 tons.

*Young, Mrs. M., Alexander Valley.*—Total, 4 acres; all in bearing; soil gravelly loam; valley; southern exposure; crop, 10 tons.

*Young, Michael, Healdsburg.*—Total, 7 acres; all in bearing; soil gravelly; valley; southern exposure; crop, 15 tons.

*Zalfo, G., Cloverdale.*—Total, 15 acres; all in bearing; soil black loam; valley; southern exposure; crop, 50 tons.

---

# FIFTH DISTRICT.

COMPRISING THE TOWNSHIPS OF BODEGA, OCEAN, REDWOOD, AND SALT POINT.

---

*Austin, Granville T., Guerneville.*—Total, 12 acres; all in bearing; soil red loam; mountain, summit land; exposure, level land on top of high hills; crop, 40 tons.

*Beadle, Louis, Occidental.*—Total, 10 acres; all wine grapes and all in bearing; soil sandy loam; upland; northern exposure; crop, 10 tons.

*Brain, William, Occidental.*—Total, 7 acres; all in bearing; soil black loam; upland; northern exposure; crop, 17 tons.

*Bones, William, Occidental.*—Total, 12 acres; all in bearing; soil red; upland; exposure, northeast; crop, 20 tons.

*Chenoweth, J. H., Occidental.*—Total, 14 acres; all in bearing; soil light sandy loam, yellow clay below; upland; exposure, nearly level; crop, 32 tons, rotted.

*Cox, John J., Cazadero.*—Total, 12 acres; all in bearing; soil light gravelly; mountain; southern exposure; crop, 40 tons.

*Crispi, Joseph, Occidental.*—Total, 12 acres; all in bearing; soil sandy loam; upland; southern exposure; crop, 40 tons.

*Devine, Peter, Guerneville.*—Total, 8 acres; all in bearing; soil gravelly; mountain; southerly exposure; crop, 15 tons.

*Drago, Nelson, Occidental.*—Total, 21 acres; all in bearing; soil black loam; upland; eastern exposure; crop, 45 tons; cooperage, oak, 1,200 gallons.

*Dupont, James, Occidental.*—Total, 11 acres; all in bearing; soil sandy loam; upland; exposure, nearly level; crop, 20 tons.

*Fisk, J. C. & Son, ————.*—Total, 5 acres; in wine grapes, 4 acres; in raisin grapes, 1 acre; soil gravelly; mountain; crop, 6 tons; wine on hand, 100 gallons; cooperage, oak, 300 gallons.

*Francisco, Alphonso, Occidental.*—Total, 5 acres; all in bearing; soil sandy loam; upland; exposure east; crop, 12 tons.

*Gallagher, John, Occidental.*—Total, 20 acres; all in bearing; soil sandy loam; upland; exposure, slopes mostly to the south; crop, 50 tons.

*Hausmann, E. A., Occidental.*—Total, 7 acres; all in bearing; soil sandy loam; upland; exposure, all directions; crop, 10 tons; wine on hand, 150 gallons; cooperage, oak, 400 gallons.

*Hopper, Thomas, Occidental.*—Total, 30 acres; all in bearing; soil sandy loam; upland; exposure east; crop, 40 tons.

*Joost, Jacob, Guerneville.*—Total, 15 acres; all in bearing; soil red gravelly; mountain; southern exposure; crop, 30 tons.

*Kloppenberg, William, Occidental.*—Total, 12 acres; all in bearing; soil sandy loam; upland; exposure, southeast slope; crop, 48 tons.

*Korbel Brothers, Guerneville.*—Total, 220 acres; all in bearing; soil red and black loam; part valley and part hill; southern exposure; crop, 500 tons; wine on hand, 400,000 gallons; cooperage, oak, 400,000 gallons; redwood, 100,000 gallons.
This winery is nearly new. It is of brick, and is believed to be admirably adapted to the purpose for which it was intended. The large vineyard is in good condition, there being no disease in it or in any of the neighboring vineyards.

*Lancel, E. (estate of), Occidental.*—Total, 60 acres; all in bearing; soil gravelly adobe; upland; exposure, all directions; crop, 120 tons; was unable to get figures in regard to amount of wine on hand or cooperage of Lancel winery; cooperage estimated at 120,000 gallons.

*Ludolf, H., Occidental.*—Total, 20 acres; all in bearing; soil sandy loam, yellow; upland; exposure, level, on top of hill; crop, 90 tons; cooperage, oak, 3,500 gallons; redwood, 5,500 gallons.
From choice selected grapes Mr. Ludolf made at home 5,500 gallons of wine, most of which is still on hand.

*Marelli, Josette, Occidental.*—Total, 18 acres; all in bearing; soil sandy loam; mountain; exposure, nearly level; crop, 20 tons; young vineyard.

*Mathias, Paul, Santa Rosa* (vineyard near Guerneville).—Total, 6 acres; all in bearing and all wine grapes; soil light sandy; mountain; eastern exposure; crop, 15 tons.

*Nolan, C. P., Occidental.*—Total, 30 acres; all in bearing; soil light sandy loam; upland; exposure, southeast slope; crop, 85 tons.

*Prosek, Joseph, Guerneville.*—Total, 85 acres; in wine grapes; in bearing, 30 acres; soil light loam; upland; south and east exposure; crop, 24 tons; wine on hand, 5,000 gallons; cooperage, oak, 6,000 gallons.
Mr. Prosek has a very fine young vineyard just coming into bearing. He makes a choice wine, which commands a high price in the market.

*Rickseker, L. E., Santa Rosa.*—Winery is near Occidental. Total, 10 acres; all in bearing; soil red gravelly; mountain; southern exposure; crop, 15 tons.

*Ridenhour, T. W., Guerneville.*—Total, 15 acres; in wine grapes, 8 acres; in table grapes, 7 acres; soil gravelly and clay loam; upland; south and east exposure, well protected from wind; crop, 65 tons.

*Schlake, C., Occidental.*—Total, 11 acres; all in bearing; soil brown loam; upland; exposure, almost level; crop, 40 tons.

*Spechler, Richard, Occidental.*—Total, 6 acres; all in bearing; soil sandy clay, deep; mountain; exposure southeast; crop, 15 tons; wine on hand, 900 gallons; cooperage, oak, 750 gallons.
Mr. Spechler is experimenting with Riparia and Californica; vines doing well.

*Stewart, William, Occidental.*—Total, 15 acres; all in bearing; soil sandy loam; upland; exposure, level; crop, 40 tons; makes wine of part; wine on hand, 4,000 gallons; cooperage, redwood, 4,000 gallons.

*Stotz, Chas., Occidental.*—Total, 22 acres; all in bearing; soil red loam, part limestone and slate rock; mountain; exposure east and south; crop, 35 tons; wine on hand, 3,000 gallons; cooperage, oak, 4,000 gallons.

*Torrance, J. L., Guerneville.*—Total, 6 acres; all in bearing; soil dark gravelly loam; upland; exposure east and southeast; crop, 10 tons.

*Urban, Vincens, Guerneville.*—Total, 15 acres; all in bearing; soil light loam; upland; exposure west and north; crop, 16 tons; wine on hand, 800 gallons; cooperage, oak, 800 gallons. New place; first manufacturing.

*Wehrspon, A., Guerneville*—Total, 16 acres; all in bearing; soil light loam; upland; exposure south; crop, 35 tons.